IN THE TRACKS OF THE MOON HARE

Exploring the Inner Life through Imagery

CATHERINE COX MA

OMARACH PRESS

Title: In The Tracks of the Moon Hare
       Exploring the Inner Life through Imagery

Author: Catherine Cox

Cover Design & Layouts: Joanna Hassam

Publisher: Omarach Press
Website: www.omarach-press.com
First published in 2022 by Omarach Press
Edition: 1st ed.

ISBN: Paperback -978-0-6456223-0-0 E-Book - 978-0-6456223-1-7
Subjects: Spirituality, Religion

DEDICATION

This book is dedicated
to my parents,
Margaret and Graham Cox
- the kindest people I know.

TABLE OF CONTENTS

PART THREE - GRACE

FOREWORD

First there is the night. Then images come to us. This is a book from the realm of the Moon Goddess. It is a guide to visual wisdom.

Catherine Cox takes us into memorable landscapes that invite inner exploration. Drawing on her own experiences with enchantment, she tells vivid stories to stir the imagination and evoke emotional resonances with invisible energies.

This gentle tour of the lands of memories, dreams and stories deepens our understanding of our own spiritual journeys. There is timeless knowledge to be discovered in these pages. This lovely book will take you away from the routine of everyday life to a place of quiet reflection.

Joseph Campbell taught us to read the picture language. Catherine Cox reveals how imagery can show us the treasures of the soul.

There are times to revisit the deeper places. Accounts of entering a mysterious reality behind our everyday world appear in every culture. Catherine draws guidance from these narratives that show the way along universal stages on the path to illumination.

A big step is noticing the abundance of symbolism all around us, hiding in plain sight. Catherine shows how reflective practices, such as Guided Imagery, can reveal secrets that give life more meaning. Her ear has been close to the heartbeat of the archetypal Unconscious.

'*In the Tracks of the Moon Hare*' is a prize for the earnest seeker. It passes along a shamanic elixir brought back from other states of being.

JONATHAN YOUNG, PHD,
PSYCHOLOGIST
Founding Curator,
Joseph Campbell Archives

ACKNOWLEDGEMENTS

No creative project is the work of a single person - this book is no different. I would like to thank a number of people who have provided feedback but also heart-felt encouragement to me during the process of writing and editing this book. To Lynne Leslie, Amy Adams, Fran Stafford and Neil Wallace - thank you, from the bottom of my heart.

To Dr Jonathan Young - it is difficult for me to adequately express my gratitude for your insight and wisdom but also your willingness to offer your guidance in such a generous way.

And last but by no means least, to Peter Briers - your love and support day by day has kept me going with this project when I was ready to give up. You have made it possible for me to fulfil a life-long ambition - to become a published author.

PREFACE

Imagine: The night is dark and although your eyes are adjusting it is difficult to see quite where you are. There are dense shapes nearby, their outlines fuzzy. Are they monsters, waiting to trip you if you stray off the path? Long shapes like skinny arms reach out to you - you do your best to avoid them and keep moving. It is disorienting and disquieting, everything around you a vague hint of what might lay hidden.

The path you are following is only just discernible. You stop walking, stand where you are, close your eyes for a moment and wait. Your breathing slows down, the perfect stillness of the night seeps into you.

And then it happens - the moon gently emerges from behind her veil of clouds, illuminating the glorious landscape all around you. The arms which threatened to seize you are the branches of an enormous ancient Hornbeam. What you thought were monsters are boulders marking the edge of your path.

Then just ahead you notice tiny silver marks, only visible now with the Moon's touch. Carefully, steadily, quietly, you follow them, off the path and into a field. The grass shimmers for a moment as a soft breeze passes. And then all is perfectly still once again.

1

The tracks are not so easy to follow but the longer you walk the more familiar this territory seems to become. Then at last you see him gazing lovingly up at his Goddess, bathing in her light..... The Moon Hare.

In the brief passage above I have endeavoured to create something which hints at what I see as the essence of this book. I have begun with Imagery because we are entering an imaginal landscape - exploring ways in which to access the mysterious but beautiful world which lies within each and every one of us. Metaphorical interpretations of the moon and the symbolic image of the mythical 'Moon Hare' encapsulate so much of what I wish to express. The moon I imagined as I wrote this passage was glorious, its light all-encompassing yet gentle.

The light where I grew up in Australia can be incredibly harsh. At times it can seem as though there is no hiding from it. It is brilliant and it can be white hot. There is a very famous poem by Dorothea MacKellar which children of my generation all learned at school. The second stanza begins: 'I love a sunburnt country, a land of sweeping plains, of ragged mountain ranges, of droughts and flooding rains.' (1) The expression 'a sunburnt country' is etched into the shared cultural consciousness in Australia with very good reason.

In February 2000 I left Australia and moved to the Isle of Skye, just off the west coast of Scotland. Skye is an incredibly special place - magical, beautiful, wild. The landscape I came to know there could not have been more different from the sub-tropical region in which I grew up. I went from extreme heat and humidity to snow and ice; from rainforest and beaches to bleak but beautiful mountains.

But there is also a different quality of light on Skye than I had previously known and it took me by surprise - it is light with an incredible scope of variety, from the soft diffuse tones of Autumn to the long gentle light nights of mid-summer. At these times blackout blinds were a must - twilight would last until almost midnight in June. And frankly I had never before experienced such dark winter nights as I did in the Highlands of Scotland. I now live in a rural area in southern Tasmania, an island off the south coast of Australia. We live a long way from the nearest town - even the neighbours are hidden from view. Winter nights here are certainly very dark but they are nowhere near as dense as the darkness of the winter nights I experienced in the far north of Skye.

Once Autumn came to the Highlands and those dark nights closed in, I would sometimes choose not to close the blinds, the dense night a kind of comforting blanket. There were some nights though when the light from the moon was so bright and the sky so clear I would wake up. Broken sleep can naturally be annoying, debilitating, even depressing. But on those nights I would get up and just spend some time looking out at the beauty of the moon and that velvet night sky. If the angle was right I would sometimes have the added blessing of seeing the moon's reflection in the water of the loch which was just a hundred meters or so down the hill from where I lived.

* * * * * *

One night I was even more blessed: the moon took on the guise of a 'Moon Goddess' and stepped right into one of my dreams. She took me by the hand and we flew up into that glorious night sky, past ominous patches of dense fog. She warned me not to become distracted by those - they were irrelevant. We kept flying upwards until the sky was crystal clear and I could absorb the stillness and beauty around me. I had never had a vision quite like it! The numinous, magical quality of that dream has inspired and sustained me more than I can possibly express in mere words.

But the most inspiring part of this dream was that it occurred during a very difficult period in my life. I was quite depressed, but even worse than that was that I felt utterly lost - I had absolutely no idea how to make the changes I knew I needed to make. Despite that, or perhaps because things were so challenging at that time, I awoke the next morning feeling the first seeds of real hope taking hold within my heart, in the deepest part of my being.

This was the first time that I had really understood that there is an incredible resource available to each of us in the richness of stories and symbols, myth, poetry and dreams. The Moon in my dream really was a light in the darkness, guiding me forwards when I could not see further than the next few weeks; when, frankly, I had absolutely no idea where I was going in my life.

The dream was also incredibly practical. It acutely articulated the direction of my studies, something I had only had a vague feeling about up until then. Eventually I enrolled in a Masters programme majoring in Transformational Psychology. This is a school of psychology which explores where psychology and the wisdom traditions meet. I had studied some Developmental Psychology as part of my first degree to become a teacher, but this was another world altogether! I immersed myself in the concepts of Jungian Depth Psychology, Symbolic Imagery, Mythology and Folklore and slowly but surely things began to click for me. One of the most inspiring things I learned was how symbols bypass the gatekeeper of one's rational mind and speak directly to the quiet places deep within.

There is a beautiful little book by Clarissa Pinkola Estes called "Warming the Stone Child". One theme she explores is that of the gift of intuition and the internal guidance we all possess. To quote Dr Estes: *".... all of those in the Arts who live so close with their ear against the heartbeat of the archetypal unconscious...."* (2) In her own unique Bardic way, Dr Estes is expressing something poignant and mysterious - a quality which is inherent in the nature of symbolic Imagery, whether that be in folk tales, dreams, movies, meditations, or even the Tarot.

Keeping our ears close to the 'heartbeat of the unconscious' is what this book is about. Although artists are often able to do this instinctively, we all of us have this connection - we can all pay attention to that heartbeat. It sings its way through stories and dreams, it is present in poetry and art. Its mystery is that it is personal but also transpersonal, unique yet also shared. It is expressed through the language of Symbolic Imagery - the language of the Unconscious itself.

Symbolic Images are overdetermined - they are redolent with layers and layers of meaning. (3) What I didn't understand at the time of my 'Moon Dream' is one particular interpretation of the Moon as a symbol - that it is synonymous with a mysterious quality of guidance, an internal guidance which allows us to access the resources and wisdom of our own deepest heart, our own creative spirit. That guidance forms a kind of portal into the realm of magic, of the Celtic 'Otherworld', the ancestors, or what Carl Jung called the 'Collective Unconscious'. It shares insights and solutions to problems we may be wrestling with. It gives voice to the whisperings which emerge from the most creative part of our being.

The voice of that guidance is usually quiet, like a whisper when you are half asleep. You notice it and then it slips away, a subtle feeling you perhaps cannot quite name. You experience an understanding, maybe even an acute insight! ...And the next day you can't quite remember its detail. You wake up in the morning with the last tendrils of a beautiful dream weaving through your mind, yet before you can write it down, it is gone.

The voice of that guidance is very like the Moon Hare - a mythical creature only glimpsed, never caught. Indeed you may find only subtle signs of his presence. My goal in this book is to help you to find those tracks within your own heart and mind, to support you to find your way through your own internal landscape. It is Imagery which lights that path. Imagery is the language of the Unconscious and of the 'Deep Self' - what I like to call your 'heart of hearts'. That is where we are heading - through the mystery of the Unconscious into your creative spirit. Whatever your profession, your experience, your world view or your beliefs, Imagery is part of you.

* * * * * * *

In the chapters which follow I have drawn upon synchronicities, memories of special experiences in my everyday life and within my internal world, snippets from dreams, spontaneous insights which occurred during courses I have taught over the years, the blessing of some beautiful if mysterious experiences I have had in the natural world, as well as my experiences of journalling for personal reflection.

I will take you where Imagery has lead me - through liminal zones and sacred landscapes; exploring symbols and stories lush with the beauty of the Mythic

Imagination; and into the quiet magic of dreams. The late priest, poet and philosopher John O'Donohue said of the internal world that: *"It has territories which extend endlessly inwards and have depths that are ancient"*. (4) The beautiful language of Imagery, however it is expressed, is what guides you through that territory.

I hope that you will find that exploration as enriching as I have done.

With my very best wishes

Cathy

INTRODUCTION

Imagine: It is mid-winter and night has fallen. You are dressed warmly, rugged up against the bitter cold. You are walking through the depths of a beautiful forest. There is snow all around, banked up against the trees, muffling any sound. It is so cold that the air seems to crystallise as you breathe it in. The glimpses of sky you can see through the canopy of trees is crystal clear, the stars and moon lighting your way. The moon is so bright, reflected on the snow, so you can find your way easily. The night air is still, and so, so quiet. You hear an owl a little way away but then the stillness and the quiet descend once again.

Up ahead there is a cottage, soft golden light coming from its windows and smoke rising from the chimney. The door is wooden but light and easy to open. This haven from the snow is incredibly inviting so you walk inside and close the door behind you.

The room you have entered is lit only with lanterns and candles - the colours create an impression of having walked inside a giant tree. There is every shade of green, from rich moss to an almost steel grey-green; there are golden browns, rich russet tones - every possible colour of autumn is spread out around you. Berry red and liquid amber, teal green and dusty pink. There is a subtle scent of woodsmoke and pine and a soft arm chair before the fire.

11

So you take off your coat and sit down, sinking into the comfort of the chair, the cushions enveloping you, the warmth from the fire seeping into your bones. Your breathing slows down and becomes more and more relaxed and gentle. The crackle of the fire is the only sound you notice - everything else is completely still.

Your eyelids begin to droop - you are incredibly relaxed. So you sit here for a while, wrapped in the colours and scents of the forest and you rest.

Take a few moments to re-imagine the scene above. Picture yourself walking through the snow; imagine what the fire would smell like; conjure up how it would feel to sink into the chair and feel warmth seeping back into your cold hands.

That is Imagery.

I believe our capacity for Imagery to be one of the richest and most mysterious aspects of human consciousness. Stephen Larsen, an American mythologist, describes it as *'an aboriginal language: the universal tongue of the human imagination.'* (5)

So what exactly is Imagery and how does it work?

The fundamental mechanism of Imagery, that is, how it actually works, is still a mystery. It does seem to be a natural language, a vital part of the nervous system and is the province of 'right brain' thinking. Through the Nobel Prize winning work of Dr Roger Sperry we know that the two hemispheres of the brain 'think' differently. The left-brain is linear and analytical; it uses words and logic and takes things apart. The right-brain thinks in pictures, sounds and feelings and it synthesises – puts things together. The left-brain is most concerned with the outer world; the right brain with the inner world of perception, insight and form.

According to Dr Martin Rossman, a leading physician and expert in Imagery:

"Essentially, it is a flow of thoughts you can see, hear, feel, smell or taste. An image is an inner representation of your experience or your fantasies, a way your mind codes, stores and expresses information. Imagery is the currency of dreams and daydreams; memories and reminiscence; plans, projections, and possibilities. It is the language of the arts, the emotions and most importantly, of the deeper self." (6)

Neuroscience and dream research tell us Imagery is a biological function - it is 'hard-wired' into us. As is the case with any other language, the more we work with Imagery, the more fluent we become and the more we are able to explore its territory - the vast expanses of the Unconscious and of the Deep Self.

There are a number of easily accessible ways in which one can explore and work with Imagery and in that way develop confidence in understanding its language.

Imagery is the language of our dreams, our own very

personal and unique gateway into the Unconscious. Our understanding of dreams today owes much to Carl Jung who analysed and theorised about his own dreams as well as those of his patients, for many years.

Imagery is the language of Myths and Folk Stories. These stories capture the universal challenges of human life - the problems which will invariably come along. The themes of these tales can be potent but they are made accessible by being presented in the events and actions of recognisable personalities, even if they are at times doing extraordinary things.

Imagery is the language of the Tarot. Look at any one of the thousands of different Tarot decks available today and you will discover instantly recognisable characters and experiences. There is incredible variety in the stories and belief systems upon which the cards are based but there are parallels too - consistent symbols and symbolic elements, regardless of the context in which the artist has portrayed them.

Imagery is the language upon which many meditations and relaxations are based, that is, Guided Imagery. Guided Imagery is used these days in all sorts of contexts - Meditation; Self-healing and relaxation; even in elite sport. There is no doubt it is a powerful tool with which to overcome obstacles, find solutions and develop one's creativity.

Every time you reflect on your dreams, listen to or read a mythic story, engage in Guided Imagery, or look at a Tarot image, something quite magical is occurring. Those stories, meditations and cards comprise a synthesis of symbols which are communicating directly with your Unconscious. Imagery may spark off feelings deep within you, sometimes potent, sometimes subtle. If you allow it to do so, it can lead you into mysterious yet incredibly fertile territory, whilst somehow also lighting your path.

The crucial aspect when working with Imagery in any form is that its potency lies in allowing its message to reach you gently, perhaps even obliquely. Each of the pathways explored in this book suggest ways to become receptive to those messages - the insight which emerges from those resources of the psyche which simply don't operate within the framework of rational thought.

To begin with though it is necessary to paint a backdrop, against which those pathways will make more sense...

PART ONE - BACKDROP

CHAPTER 1 - RETREAT

Most of us live our lives these days immersed in the digital world, saturated in information and constantly connected to the wider world through our mobile phones, computers and various 'devices'. Our easy access to information is wonderful but the cacophony of words and ideas can at times threaten to overwhelm us. One of the most crucial steps to take if you wish to access the Unconscious, is to find ways in which to cocoon yourself from the noise of everyday life, and especially digital 'noise'.

The digital connection we have to the wider world is two-way. More than ever before the boundaries between work and our private lives have been blurred. Many employers seem to expect that folk should be accessible at any time of the day or night, even during official 'vacation' time. Shops are open 7 days a week and well into the night, some of them 24 hours a day. Of course there is also internet shopping which can naturally occur at any time. And running a small business often requires a much greater commitment than its owner may have anticipated. The demands on our attention these days can be insidious, draining and in some cases, unhealthy in the extreme. We all really do need some time to 'unplug'!

We have witnessed too an extraordinary rise in the popularity of Retreat Centres and Meditation classes since the turn of the Millennium. This isn't surprising given the way in which phone technology has evolved during the same period, and especially so since the advent of the 'Smart Phone'. Many folk recognise that some aspects of their lives have become out of balance. They are instinctively seeking out the space they need. A good holiday is an absolute joy and attending a retreat might just give you a taste of what it is you crave. It is clear though too that many places which call themselves 'Retreat Centres' are actually offering *courses* in a range of activities - meditation, Yoga, Reiki etc - rather than an opportunity for genuine Retreat. Some centres offer little more than Spa or Wellness programmes. There is obviously nothing wrong with these courses or programmes. Caring for yourself physically, having some holistic treatments, practising yoga or meditation - these can be healthy and enjoyable. But practising yoga and eating vegan food for a few days does not necessarily mean you have been 'on retreat'.

I do not say this lightly. I was privileged to run a Retreat Centre on the Isle of Skye for almost 7 years. Like most of the Highlands and Islands of Scotland, Skye is an incredibly beautiful place and much of it is still an unspoiled wilderness. The experience of retreat in such a location gets under your skin and remarkably quickly. I witnessed first hand the palpable relief in visitors as they began to sink into the peacefulness that such a location offers, the 'Peace of Wild things' as poet Wendell Berry so beautifully expresses it:

> *I come into the peace of wild things*
> *who do not tax their lives with forethought*
> *of grief. I come into the presence of still water.*

And I feel above me the day-blind stars
waiting with their light. For a time
I rest in the grace of the world, and am free. (7)

(You will find this poem in its entirety in the Appendix at the end of this book.)

There was an aura of hopefulness in guests as they shook my hand, about to return to their everyday lives and routines, backs a little straighter, genuine smiles in their eyes.

Yet the peaceful locations in which many Retreat Centres are situated isn't really the most significant aspect of a 'Retreat' as I understand it - the location isn't really the point.

Consider some common definitions of the word 'Retreat':

*   A quiet or secluded place in which one can rest and relax
*   Withdraw to a quiet or secluded place
*   To go away from a person or place to escape from fighting or danger.

The first two points above are self-explanatory. But the third - well this meaning I find most significant of all. In the context of anxiety, depression, burnout and other stress-related illnesses and their prevalence, there really is danger and it is acute. If *Retreat* can only happen in a specific kind of place and a remote place at that, does that mean we can never escape from the very real danger of stress-related illnesses? Can we only hope to avoid them for a time? What an appalling and hopeless thought!

The deeper purpose of *Retreat* I think becomes much more apparent when you think of 'Retreat' as a verb rather than as a noun. This is a simple (but not necessarily easy) shift in one's mindset - to find the time and, more importantly, the motivation to retreat from the world and all of its demands, to turn inwards and listen to the quiet voice which emerges from one's deepest heart.

In his 2018 book 'In Praise of Wasting Time', author and MIT Professor Alan Lightman explores recent trends and studies into the mental health challenges which seem to have grown considerably worse during the digital age.

"I believe I have lost something of my inner self - the part of me that imagines, that dreams, that explores, that is constantly questioning who I am and what is important to me…. When I listen to my inner self, I hear the breathing of my spirit. Those breaths are so tiny and delicate, I need stillness to hear them, I need slowness to hear them. I need vast, silent spaces in my mind." (8)

This is an aspect of *Retreat* which each of us can access from the comfort of home, even if that home is in the midst of a city. All that is really required is a particular mindset and the will to develop a practice of reflection - to learn to recognise the wisdom which arises from within, even when that occurs in subtle, oblique ways. The key is to prioritise that space, even if only for a few minutes - to make it special in some way. Joseph Campbell, the great 20th century mythologist, called this space a 'sacred place'.

In a series of interviews called 'The Power of Myth', journalist Bill Moyers asked Campbell: 'What does it mean to have a sacred place?' This was Campbell's reply:

"This is an absolute necessity for anybody today. You must have a room, or a certain hour or so a day, where you don't know who your friends are, you don't know what you owe anybody, you don't know what anybody owes to you. This is a place where you can simply experience and bring forth what you are and what you might be. This is the place of creative incubation. At first you may find that nothing happens there. But if you have a sacred place and use it, something eventually will happen. (9)

Campbell was speaking in 1987 - how much more of a necessity this kind of sacred place has become today!

Discovering or creating a sacred place into which you can regularly immerse yourself can begin to redress the debilitating imbalance so common in our lives today. If you do not subscribe to a particular spiritual belief system, try not to be put off by the word 'sacred'. Creating a sacred place for yourself and developing a practice of reflection is important whether you have particular spiritual beliefs or not. In fact this practice doesn't necessarily have anything to do with religion or beliefs, though you may choose to use it that way. It simply needs to be a place or a time in which you can be 'held' - a place for what Campbell called 'creative incubation'; a place or a time in which you can let go of all your day-to-day concerns and give your attention to that mysterious inner world.

This place needn't be inside your home, or a church or other formal religious place. You may find that going for a walk in a favourite landscape is incredibly special to you; perhaps you are blessed to live near the sea and love nothing better than to sit and gaze at the horizon, even if only for a few minutes. You might have a particular time of day in which you are able to deeply relax and let go of your worries - first thing in the morning or late at night, the blanket of darkness softening the sharp edges of your anxieties.

The only element I would suggest you build into your time in your sacred place is quiet. I do not just mean in your environment alone - I mean a sense of quiet in your body and in your mind, to let go of distractions even for a few minutes. The silence is likely to feel uncomfortable, at least to begin with. This is not surprising as we seem to be rapidly pushing it out of our lives.

"Silence is the voice of mystery. Silence lets us dream again." (10)

Finding or creating your own 'Sacred Place' is fundamental to effectively building pathways to the Unconscious. Whatever you choose for your 'sacred place', it needs to be nourishing and special enough to help you to access that beautiful and mysterious world within. To quote Hermann Hesse, a Swiss poet, novelist and artist:

"Within you, there is a stillness and a sanctuary to which you can retreat at any time and be yourself." (11)

CHAPTER 2 - EDGES

CHAPTER SIX

Have you noticed that strange 'in between' state just as you are waking up in the morning? You are no longer asleep but you are not fully awake yet either. You may notice snippets from your dreams in this state before they dissolve like a morning mist. This is a *Liminal State of Consciousness* and it forms a bridge to your Unconscious.

The word liminal comes from the Latin root limen which means 'a position on the threshold,' or a place 'betwixt and between'. When you are in this state you are in a very special zone in which quite magical experiences can occur.

You may recognise this state if you have been absorbed in a beautiful musical performance; whilst meditating or exercising; perhaps you have been totally absorbed in an activity such as a hobby or craft or simply walking on the beach. You are awake but very relaxed - musing or day-dreaming. You cannot simply make this state of mind happen. You can however cultivate those qualities which will allow it to arise.

This is a state of mind from which powerful insights emerge or through which you may discover solutions to problems with which you have been wrestling, perhaps for some time.

Working with Imagery in all its forms pulls you into this liminal zone.

We are all blessed with the capacity to drift in our mind into a liminal space, to be open to the blessings of the wisdom and insight which will meet us there, bubbling up from within. The more you work with Imagery over time, the more you will get to know this internal imaginal landscape and the more you will find yourself moving into it at other times - not only in the moment when you are actually focused on doing so - meditating or journalling. When this is likely to occur is quite personal. I have found over time that I am likely to slip into this liminal space when I am in nature or visiting an ancient site.

There was a particularly magical experience I had recently when the reality of this liminal state was very clear for me. In April of 2019 I was fortunate to be able to visit 'Flag Fen', not far from Peterborough in the south-east of England. In the mid 1980s archeologist Francis Pryor discovered the remains of a kilometre long prehistoric timber causeway at Flag Fen. This causeway across the marshes was used for hundreds of years as a sacred place - a place to make offerings, appeal to the ancestors, gods and goddesses - the deities of that time and place. Hundreds of votive offerings were found during the archeological dig which followed his discovery.

I had wanted to visit Flag Fen since I had first learned about it some years before. I was fascinated and excited as I entered the 'Preservation Hall' - a structure which has been erected over a particularly well preserved section of the causeway. But nothing could have prepared me for the wonder I experienced as I looked down into the water at those 3000+ year old timbers. In that moment time and modernity fell away. Though the room was dark there was a subtle sparkle on the surface of the water. Though utterly still there was a mysterious dynamism present. I was absolutely in awe! I could have been a pre-historic woman looking into that mysterious world, standing at the boundary between our world and the Celtic Otherworld.

As I stood there I couldn't have explained rationally what I was experiencing. That is actually the point - the experience was one in which my being had moved spontaneously from the rational and logical into something else, as if a portal had actually opened in front of me. I began to have an inkling, just the beginning of a subtle feeling, about why human beings have gazed into lakes and pools and have prayed at the edge of holy wells for thousands of years. In the quiet of that dark room my heart was pulled into the mystery of those liminal crossing places, those gateways between worlds.

There are many of these ancient sites in the United Kingdom and Ireland. Thanks to the work of archeologists in recent decades we can be reasonably confident about certain aspects of sacred ritual in pre-historic Britain. One of the most striking characteristics is that almost always there is something of the liminal about the special places in which those sacred rituals took place. Water certainly features prominently - similar to those found at Flag Fen, offerings have been found in wells, ponds and bogs in much of the country. Particular islands in Britain have long histories of spiritual association, such as Iona off the west coast and Lindsfarne - Holy Island - in the east. But there are also extraordinary sites on tiny fresh water islands in rivers and lakes such as Inchmahome Priory in the Lake of Menteith near Stirling in Scotland and St Columba's Island in the River Snizort, a few miles from where I used to live on the Isle of Skye. Early Christian sites were almost always established in places which had been considered to be spiritually important for generations.

Ancient stone monuments such as Stonehenge, Callanish on the Isle of Lewis, the Ring of Brodga in Orkney and Newgrange in Ireland are aligned with the mid-winter Solstice. But numerous other smaller monuments - stone circles, burial mounds and so on, are aligned or contain alignments to other significant astronomical events such as equinoxes. We know too from the archeological record about the celebrations and feasts which occurred at special times, festivals such as Beltaine and Samhain. (These are more frequently known these days as 'May day' and 'Halloween'.)

The alignments of these ancient monuments to such specific times in the calendar as well as the timing of celebrations and feasts again points to the liminal. These times were seen to be special: the turning of the year; harvest times; mid-winter and mid-summer; crossing times from a season of dark and cold into a time of warmth, light and plentiful food. These were the times to seek the guidance and blessings of the ancestors, to make offerings, ask for intervention for a good crop, or for good health during the long, cold, dark winter to come.

In essence what we understand about the spiritual practices of prehistoric people points us to the idea of a continued life beyond this life, of an invisible plain behind the visible, the 'Otherworld' which was so present and dynamic - a natural part of day-to-day pre-historic life.

This invisible plain is somehow supportive of the visible one in which we, too, must live and to which we must relate. To quote Joseph Campbell again : *"I would say that is the basic theme of all mythology – that there is an invisible plane supporting the visible one."* (12)

This idea of an 'invisible plain' is also central to shamanic practices. Dr Michael Harner, a world authority on shamanism, defines the shamanic way as a method of opening a portal and entering a different reality (13). John Matthews describes the Shaman as someone who *'enters other states of being'*, and who then returns with knowledge, wisdom or healing on behalf of others. (14)

Psychology points us towards this invisible plane too. Most people these days have some understanding of the 'Unconscious'. Sigmund Freud is probably the best known early theorist to have used the concept of the Unconscious in understanding aspects of psychological life. But Carl Jung developed the understanding that the Unconscious has two distinct parts - what he called the 'Personal Unconscious' and the 'Collective Unconscious'.

The Personal Unconscious applies to the part of the psyche which most of us understand simply as 'The Unconscious' or 'Subconscious'. It consists of material which is unnecessary for our day to day needs or which perhaps is too painful or even traumatic for our conscious mind to remain consistently aware of in our waking state. Our defences work to keep these troubling elements out of consciousness, at least at first. (15) Much of this content arises from personal experience - it is biographical.

The 'Collective Unconscious' Jung saw as a *transpersonal* field of consciousness to which we are all connected - it is *beyond* the personal. His understanding was that we are connected to this transpersonal field even if we are not aware of that connection in our waking lives.

There is an extraordinary phenomenon in which people experience dreams rich in Imagery which makes no sense to them in the context of their everyday life. Sometimes these dreams reflect gods and goddesses which may be quite alien to the way the Divine is personified in the dreamer's own spiritual paradigm; for example the dreamer may have grown up in a traditional western home but they experience dreams about Egyptian gods, Maori legends, ancient pagan goddesses. Indeed at times somebody who is an avowed atheist may have a dream rich in overtly spiritual Imagery. In most of these cases, the dreams are reported as being incredibly powerful emotional experiences - experiences which are numinous. These sorts of instances support the notion of a 'Collective Unconscious' to which we are all connected, even though that connection remains elusive when sought through rational thought alone.

I would describe my experience at Flag Fen as numinous - a subjective experience of the Divine. It was spontaneous - I had not sought any kind of special encounter such as I experienced. What I have discovered though is that the more you enter into the liminal, the thinner the veil between your waking consciousness and the Unconscious will become.

Edges - these liminal spaces - are incredibly rich, fertile places. This is the case in everything from modern Permaculture cultivation practices to dream analysis. These liminal places are indistinct - porous. Whether they occur at a boundary of seasons or place, or moving from the world of sleep and dreams into the dawn of wakefulness on a new morning, that boundary - that liminal zone - is special. Our ancestors clearly understood this - they invested ENORMOUS energy as communities to build sacred landscapes and perform rituals centred upon the reality of just how special these places and times were.

Practising how to enter this liminal state will build a pathway for you to the riches of your Unconscious. It is through being able to enter a liminal state that we can begin to gain access to this extraordinary world and its infinite wisdom.

The magic of Imagery, whether expressed through our dreams, mythic stories, meditations, or the Tarot, is that it sits right at that boundary, on the edge between the rational and the intuitive, between logic and poetry.

CHAPTER 3 - MYTH

"Once upon a time, in such and such a place, something happened." (15)

Human beings tell stories. It is an incredibly powerful way for us to organise and share our experiences. Children will begin telling or re-telling stories by the time they are about 2 years old. Ultimately we use stories to make sense of the world and our place within it.

Stories envelop us - narrative permeates much of our day-to-day reality. Advertisers have long understood how to use a story to sell; politicians certainly understand narrative and how to create the kind of story to win them power. They have even become skilled at doing so in 280 characters. We tell ourselves stories - all the time. Stories to fit our beliefs; stories to understand our experiences, when we have been hurt or have experienced something exciting.

It would seem story-telling is universal. Human beings have told stories since pre-history and we still tell them, regardless of the culture or the times in which we live. And those stories are much more than mere entertainment. In ancient times, long before literacy became the province of the common man, when the community wanted to pass along wisdom and important knowledge gained through the experience of their forebears, they did so by way of stories (16).

These particular stories are those we have inherited as myths and folk tales - stories which capture the universal challenges of human life, the problems which will invariably come along, as well as ways in which to respond to those problems. We can learn so much from these mythic tales but especially that we are part of something 'bigger' - giants, monsters and powerful magical beings can step into our lives at any time in a story, bringing with them events beyond our control. Life is much bigger than us and these tales teach of our need to live with courage, that life at times may demand that we transcend the limits of what we understand about ourselves, in order to grow, thrive and succeed. All in all: *"Mythology has to do with how to live."* (17)

It is vital though to understand that myths and folk tales are not mere teaching stories - they are so much more than that! Many carry guidance and life lessons, sometimes quite explicitly and directly. But what I personally find intriguing is that the guidance is more often carried implicitly, embedded into the characters and events of the story, the gods and goddesses, relationships and wars, even the landscape in which these events take place. The wisdom in these tales is clothed in metaphoric, poetic language - its magic is that it speaks directly to the more mysterious parts of us which lie deep within.

The challenge though is that in the Western world of the 21st century we have inherited an habitual bias in our way of thinking - a bias towards engaging with life and the world around us in a fundamentally rational way.

THE LOSS OF MYTH

Rational thought is a fantastic gift which lies at the root of the technological miracles we take for granted. But there is no doubt that relying a little too heavily on rational thought alone means that we risk losing something precious.

This rather one-sided way of engaging with the world wasn't always the norm. Most pre-modern cultures recognised two distinct modes of thinking - the ancient Greeks called them *Logos* and *Mythos*. Logos (logical or rational thought) and Mythos (the Mythic Imagination) were not perceived as being in conflict, nor was one seen to be superior to the other. They were understood as being complementary.

Logos essentially refers to rational thinking - that which is required to engage with the external world: to make tools, build houses, develop technologies, organise communities and to improve our physical quality of life. But the human psyche does not simply operate rationally. Logos cannot help us to deal with grief, to seek wisdom, to express love, or to find meaning in our lives. For these sorts of experiences we need a fundamentally different way of thinking - *Mythos*.

Mythos is a mode of thought which allows us to grasp absolutely fundamental truths, those mysterious aspects which bring meaning to our lives. We experience these aspects best through the Mythic Imagination -

through poetry, art and music, through symbols, story and metaphor.

Below is a beautiful quote from the 1989 movie "Dead Poet's Society" in which Robin William's character, Mr Keating, is speaking to his students about the significance of poetry:

"We read and write poetry because we are members of the human race. And the human race is filled with passion. Medicine, law, business, engineering, these are noble pursuits and necessary to sustain life. But poetry, beauty, romance, love, these are what we stay alive for." (18)

The success of Logos, of rational thought, science and technology, is evident all around us and there is absolutely nothing wrong with that. Everything from cars to the internet, medical science to a flushing toilet we have, primarily, thanks to Logos. Science and technology have revolutionised our way of life.

I think it is a little sad though, that in our technologically brilliant world we tend to misunderstand Mythos. The term 'Myth' has even come to describe something which isn't true. To quote Joseph Campbell:

"The word myth now means falsehood, and so we have lost the symbols and that mysterious world of which they speak." (19)

Even more significantly, I believe we have perhaps also become a little starved of things 'mythic' - our need for it neglected. At the very least many of us have lost touch with it or have forgotten quite how to access this mode of thinking - we no longer find it so easy to access the Mythic Imagination.

There is a reason that *Mythos* evolved in the human psyche alongside *Logos*. It is a natural part of each and every one of us - part of our internal language and our dreams; part of how we remember and how we express love; how we daydream and imagine and find creative solutions to the problems which come along in our lives; why we can find meaning in music and art or identify with characters in stories, even the fantastical ones.

The source of the potency of Mythos lies in its symbolism, whether in the tangible form of images or in the abstract form of ideas. This symbolism encapsulates the very stuff of life, the archetypal experiences we human beings share - birth, death, love, fear, friendship, betrayal, creativity, loss - and much more besides.

The real magic of Imagery is that without even necessarily recognising that it is happening, it will be communicating with your Unconscious mind. It speaks to some kernel *in* you. Remember Imagery is meant to be experienced as *Mythos*. Try relating to it only through rational thought and you may just miss the point. More importantly, you will miss a clue as to how to access the wisdom of your Unconscious.

You cannot reach the Unconscious by an act of will, by deciding *rationally* to do so - it simply doesn't work like that.

POPULAR CULTURE

When one looks at popular culture over the past few decades, storytelling genres with mythical themes at their core have become incredibly popular. The technology which allows for extraordinarily life-like special effects is significant in this trend but the mythic threads in these stories add potency to their appeal. Ironically, contemporary technological expertise is allowing for a more life-like experience of these enchanting worlds, especially so in the world of Virtual Reality and digital games - *Logos* meets *Mythos*.

In film: The 'Lord of the Rings' and 'Hobbit' trilogies; 'The Chronicles of Narnia'; The 'Harry Potter' and 'Fantastic Beasts' phenomena; 'Star Trek', 'Star Wars' and other science fiction stories; even the Marvel universe with its super heroes and Norse gods - these particular stories have been enormously successful and popular. In recent years there have been remakes of 'Cinderella', 'Rapunzel' and the Stephen Sondheim musical 'Into the Woods'. There are new fairy tales in 'Frozen', 'Brave' and 'Maleficent'.

On television: One of the most popular series in the West in recent years was 'Game of Thrones'; series called 'Once Upon a Time' and 'Grimm' have been successful enough to have run for a number of seasons in each case. And spin offs and origin stories from the Marvel universe abound.

Although one may question the manner in which some of our more traditional stories have been adapted the mythic thread is still present and it is still speaking to us. This fascination with the Mythic Imagination in our culture may be a sign that many in our largely secular society still yearn for a richer interior life than may be immediately apparent.

PART TWO ⊙ - PATHWAYS

In Part Two we will explore some more specific strategies for using Imagery in your day-to-day life. In Chapter 4 you will find a number of suggested Guided Imagery narratives for you to try. I have used Guided Imagery with music and without, with a recorded narrator and without - sometimes I have an idea of the kind of imaginal place I wish to explore and sometimes I do not. There is no one particular 'right way' to engage with Imagery. Perhaps it is more accurate to say that there are many 'right ways'. Allowyourself to be creative and adventurous, and record your experiences in a journal if at all possible.

In Chapter 5 we explore the world of Dreams, in Chapter 6 the Tarot and in Chapter 7 Story. Each of these is an incredibly practical expression of Imagery, especially so if explored through a practice of journalling. I cannot encourage you enough to journal about these experiences. Both your dreams and your interaction with Tarot images and mythic stories are potentially incredibly rich resources with which to explore the wisdom of your own Unconscious and what it wishes to share with you.

CHAPTER 4 - IMAGINE

The practice known as 'Active Imagination' was developed by Carl Jung. *"It (Active Imagination) is a meditation technique wherein the contents of one's unconscious are translated into images, narratives, or personified as separate entities."* (20) One particular expression of Active Imagination is Guided Imagery. It is a practice I use a great deal and one which I can wholeheartedly recommend!

Guided Imagery is a relaxation or contemplation practice in which you imagine yourself within your inner world, your inner 'Imaginal Landscape'. I have always found meditation difficult, despite working with a range of techniques. In contrast, Guided Imagery has worked incredibly well for me.

An experience of the Divine when in the natural world is something many people report. Indeed there is a great deal of poetry, art and music which has been inspired by such experiences. One of the great joys of using Guided Imagery is that one can build an *internal* landscape, perhaps even an internal 'Sacred Place'.

This sacred place may be a forest grove; perhaps you will be drawn to the edge of the sea; perhaps you will enter a crystal castle; or cross a heath to a circle of stones. You can certainly be confident that your Unconscious will guide you, regardless of what you think your spiritual beliefs may be. If you don't subscribe to particular spiritual beliefs, your Unconscious will also undoubtedly guide you into visions which are nourishing to you and the deepest part of your being.

And the more you seek to encounter this 'Otherworld', the more it will nourish you and enrich your experience in myriad ways.

I have experienced any number of occasions when a beautiful symbol has sparked off an internal journey of sorts. I have encountered wise beings, visited forests and caves full of gems, travelled to distant shores and have been shown breathtakingly beautiful things. I shared one of these 'Guided Imagery' relaxations in the Introduction, leading you through a snow covered landscape to the haven of a cottage.

What follows are a number of examples of Guided Imagery. You may find that one or more of these spark off your own internal wanderings, that you begin by imagining what I describe but then your Unconscious leads you off in a different direction. That is absolutely fine. These examples are certainly not prescriptive - they are just a guide with which to begin.

CIRCLE OF STONES

Imagine you are walking in woodland. It is a warm summer's evening; a soft cooling breeze lifts itself up every now and then, just enough to nudge the leaves in the trees around you. Time seems to slow and you recognise the call to relax more deeply and explore.

You find yourself walking beyond the trees into a field and out of the twilight. Suddenly it is very early in the morning. Dawn is breaking but a waning crescent moon still hangs in the sky. The light is soft but you can make out the landscape quite clearly. It is almost midsummer's eve, one of those beautiful liminal times when the thresholds to the Otherworld are more easily found.

In the middle of the field stands a circle of ancient stones - each seems to have its own spirit, its own character. Time doesn't really exist here, at least not as we know it. It is early morning and twilight and thousands of years ago and today, all at the same time. The soft mist of dawn dissolves around you and the shapes of the stones become clearer, more distinct. Stand just at the boundary of the circle and wait until you sense an invitation to enter. You may feel the air change, as if a window has opened and a fresh breeze blows gently around you.

Sit down within the circle and you will be able to feel the pulse of an incredible life force right there in the earth around you and humming in the stones. Imagine yourself just sitting and absorbing this vibration, allowing it to relax you but somehow also enliven you at the same time.

Take your time - stay as long as you wish. When you are ready to do so, imagine yourself standing again, thank the stones for their gifts and walk slowly back the way you came. Allow the scene to fade; dig your heels into the floor and take some slow deep breaths.

MOON

Imagine that you are on the shore of an enormous lake. It is night-time and the moon has risen into a clear dark sky. Slowly but surely your eyesight adjusts to the darkness and to the soft tones of moonlight all around you. Looking in either direction the shore is like a ribbon of silk stretching out as far as you can see. The water is perfectly still and the moon is mirrored in its surface, a shimmering reflection.

As you relax more and more deeply your doubts and worries of a few moments ago dissolve and you are calm. Time stretches out - you could be anyone at any time in the history of the earth. Past, present and future mingle in the moonlit water and as you gaze into the depths you feel the possibilities of life moving gently in your soul.

Let them lay there.

For now, simply drink in this peacefulness and allow the tension in your body to fall away. Trust that the moonlight is awakening something you already know deep within.

Take a few moments now - place your attention on the soles of your feet and your connection with the earth. Allow this scene to gently fade away. You are calm and centred, peaceful, fully alert and present. When you are ready to do so, dig your heels into the ground, take a deep breath and open your eyes.

LIBRARY

Imagine you are walking along a well worn paved path which is leading you to an old but very solid looking building. The path leads to the base of a set of stairs which in turn lead up to an enormous oak door. Though it looks too heavy to move the door opens easily as you turn the handle and give it a gentle push. Inside it is cool, and as your eyes adjust to the low light you see that there are shelves and shelves and shelves, all overflowing with books. Books of all kinds - of different widths, some leather bound, some so old you could imagine they will fall apart if you touch them; some books are little more than a few pages held together with thread. There are books for children and books full of sketches, books in strange languages and some with pages and pages of calculations.

Leading off in every direction are corridors which take you to more rooms, each filled as before with rows upon rows of books. There are cabinets too, with mechanical models, musical instruments and strange looking creatures; there are tables laid out with maps and sketches - drawings of plants and planets, stars and sea creatures. To call it a library somehow would not be enough - the air itself seems to carry voices of wisdom and learning from throughout the ages. And then you notice him - a gentleman of indeterminate age, bearded and mature. He is silent, just sitting comfortably and watching you, as you stand in the middle of the room, your mouth open in astonishment. 'Come... explore' is all he says and you head off down the first corridor together.

If you have a particular problem you are trying to solve, ask him to show you where to look and then see what happens.

Take a few moments now - place your attention on the soles of your feet and your connection with the earth. Allow this scene to gently fade away. You are calm and centred, peaceful, fully alert and present. When you are ready to do so, dig your heels into the ground, take a deep breath and open your eyes.

MARSHLAND

Imagine you are standing at the edge of a marsh. You can hear water moving gently nearby. The warmth of the sun touches your face and birdsong floats on the air. You hear only natural sounds - there are no machines, no cars or planes. You look down and see that right in front of you is a timber pathway - it stretches out in front of you, leading into the marshland. This pathway is sturdy and secure and so you begin to walk along it, right out into the marsh.

You are somehow between sky and earth, dry land and water, a mysterious dreamscape which cocoons you and keeps you safe. You can smell salt on the air, hear the water as it laps against the timbers. And in the distance is the sea, vast and majestic, eternally feeding and refreshing this quiet place.

Eventually you come to an enormous platform, like an island in the midst of the marsh. There are holes in its surface and you choose one. Imagine that you sit near the hole and gaze down into the water. The sun has lowered in the sky, the afternoon is beginning to settle around you. You are nearing a boundary when day meets night, sitting at the edge of our world, yet seeing into the Otherworld. Breathe in the quiet and look again into the water. There is still enough light for you to notice something sparkle. You can just see its outline - a beautiful sword, lying there beneath you. You are safe to reach into the water and draw out the sword. Hold it up in front of you and examine it closely. What does it look like?

What is it made of? Are there decorations, jewels or perhaps words inscribed on its surface? Notice as much detail as possible.

When you are ready to do so, return the sword to the water. It won't tarnish nor rot. It is here for you to retrieve at any time you wish to return. You stand and begin to walk back along the causeway. There is still enough light for you to see by. As you reach the end and step back onto solid ground the sun is setting and for a moment it seems as though a golden light is shining from within the earth rather than from above it.

Take a few moments now - place your attention on the soles of your feet and your connection with the earth. Allow this scene to gently fade away. You are calm and centred, peaceful, fully alert and present. When you are ready to do so, dig your heels into the ground, take a deep breath and open your eyes.

ANIMAL GUIDE

Imagine that you are in a room with a whole wall made of glass. You can see through this wall into the most beautiful natural landscape. It may be somewhere you have actually been, or a place you would like to visit. It may be a place which only exists in your imaginal world. There is a door in your glass wall - picture yourself standing up, walking over to the door and walking through into that beautiful natural landscape. Feel the warmth on your skin, notice how fresh and clean the air is. Take a few moments just to enjoy the place you have come to.

When you are ready, follow the path in front of you as it leads you further into your beautiful natural world. Look around you - Are there trees? Fields? A lake? Perhaps a beach? It is your landscape so go wherever you wish. Notice any sounds around you, any movement in the distance. Eventually you come to a protected space - a cove on your beach, perhaps trees around a clearing, a grove in the forest. You are safe to enter this space. Find somewhere to sit down and relax. You have come to this safe space to meet your animal guide. In your mind, invite your animal to come into your space. Just relax - they will come when they are ready. You may be able to sense them nearby. Feel the warmth in and around your heart that tells you someone who is a kindred spirit is close by. And then your animal guide approaches you. Look into their eyes, listen to what they have to communicate to you. Ask them questions if you wish to do so.

Your animal guide and friend will know when it is time to leave. Relax and let them go. You can meet with them at any time and call on them to support you with anything you need. When you are ready to do so, picture yourself standing up and walking back along the path you took to come to this place. Notice again any sounds, any smells, the warmth of the sun, the breeze on your skin.

Eventually you reach the doorway in your glass wall. Come back into your room and sit down. Slowly and steadily bring your awareness back into the room, wriggle your toes around and be aware of the earth beneath your feet. When you are ready to do so, dig your heels into the ground, take a deep breath in and open your eyes.

CHAPTER 5 - DREAMS

"The clarity with which certain incidents, people, and creatures remain with me from the dream world, I find amazing... All of them scorch the mind, branding their impression more vividly than their material counterparts..." (21)

Unfortunately I am one of those people who doesn't remember their dreams very often. As part of my Masters programme I studied a compulsory subject on Dreams and Dreaming. Naturally one of the major assessment pieces for this subject was centred around keeping a 'Dream Journal' - naturally! The professor, Dr Bulkley, had assured us in the first lecture that most folk do begin to remember their dreams once they form a conscious intention to do so. It is as if something in the Unconscious receives a signal and you begin to remember. It may only be snippets or vague feelings at times but the more you record these in a journal the more you are likely to remember. I did indeed discover that I remembered more and more as I journaled - there were patterns too, the repeated symbols becoming a kind of signal to my conscious mind to 'pay attention here'!

One particular thread which weaves its way through my dreams involves animals. I have been an animal lover for almost as long as I can remember. But the animals I encounter in my dreams are rarely cute and cuddly. There have been dolphins, elephants, fish and birds, but also snakes, which absolutely terrify me.

And one particularly memorable and frightening dream about a shark, which I explore a little later in this chapter.

Neuroscience tells us that dreams are 'hardwired' into us - they are part of our biology. And almost everybody dreams - there is only a relatively small number of people with brain injuries who don't dream. The question is: *why* do we dream?

Well there was another aspect which Dr Bulkely discussed during the course of those lectures which I found extraordinary - whilst many people report that they don't remember their dreams, most people have dreams they can never forget, even for years afterwards. Those are the dreams which 'scorch the mind'. Something amazing happens over time - in some way your conscious mind catches up with the wisdom of your Unconscious Dream state, uncovering layers and layers of meaning and insight in these unforgettable dreams.

It is as if the Unconscious wants to pull us forwards, help us to understand the path our lives are taking. (I am not referring here to 'precognitive' dreams - those dreams in which we see a future event. There is a great deal of evidence that some folk do experience these sorts of dreams.)

Perhaps then dreaming helps us to grow - emotionally, psychologically, even spiritually. Some very special dreams are even numinous - a deeply personal experience of the divine. These dreams arise from the deepest level of the psyche - no wonder in ancient civilisations there was a belief of some dreams being 'sent by God'.

In the Preface to this book I shared a little of my experience with one of the most beautiful dreams I have ever had. That dream was numinous, deeply moving, and it has become an inspiration to me during the years since.

There is no doubt that dreams are an incredibly rich resource to your waking life, whether you experience a numinous dream or not. Working with Imagery and getting to know your own personal symbolic language will undoubtedly support you in understanding your dreams. I have found that it has become a kind of short-hand and has helped me to recognise themes in the stories of my dreams - to decipher multiple meanings in the layers of symbols offered up in the night.

In the pages which follow I share a further two of my own dreams. The first was extremely frightening at the time but years later it motivated a burst of creativity from which I wrote a short story. (I have included this story in the Appendix at the end of the book.)

Finally I share what was actually more of a brief vision which occurred while I was awake. I then entered into some lucid dreaming with which to discover more of what that vision had to tell m

SHARK - DECEMBER 1999

'I am walking along a jetty at the marina where my parents keep their little boat. It is a beautiful day - clear blue skies, warm rather than hot, a slight breeze. I stop for a moment and close my eyes, my face turned towards the sun and I breathe in the salt air. I open my eyes again and look at the water. Something catches my attention - a slight movement or a sparkle on the water's surface. I lean over the edge of the jetty to look into the water and an enormous shark leaps out, vertical, just as a dolphin would do. I wake up absolutely terrified and with my heart pounding - I find I am already sitting up in bed.'

Fortunately I have very few nightmares or such frightening dreams. At the time I had this dream I had not yet started to learn about symbolism or Imagery - my knowledge of the Unconscious and how it works was minimal. And this dream was very frightening. I was breathless and my heart really was racing - the dream pulled me almost violently from my sleep. In those days I was actually a bit frightened of exploring the Unconscious and my dreams in particular. Quite ironic really, given the direction my life has taken since. I assumed at the time the shark largely represented that fear. The association with dolphins seemed simple too as I had loved dolphins since I was a child. They were something of a totem for me - I had a number of dolphin statues in my home during this period.

One of the abiding mysteries of dreams though is how many layers of meaning and insight they offer us over time. Whilst there were other understandings I have had over the years, there was one particular interpretation which I only understood relatively recently. In part, the dream was warning me about a predatory and abusive person I began working with in the months just after I had this dream. I am sad to say that I didn't have the self-knowledge to recognise this at the time and I had some incredibly difficult experiences until I was ultimately able to extricate myself from that situation.

Even more mysterious though is that such a powerful dream may have internal parallels. Most of us can identify with not exactly being on our own side, at least not all the time. The 'Inner Critic' is very real for many folk and I am no exception. Clarissa Pinkola Estes in her wonderful book 'Women who Run with the Wolves' explores this phenomenon in some detail. In particular:

"...both within and without there is a force which will act in opposition to the instincts of the natural Self, and that malignant force is what it is..." (22)

Most of us need to learn how to recognise such destructive patterns, both within and without. Yet another beautiful mystery in dreams is that they will shine a light on external and internal threats simultaneously!

It is really interesting too for me to reflect now on how much my relationship to my dreams has changed over time and especially so given how much working with Imagery of various kinds has helped me to understand the symbolism in my dreams. As you work with that language, remember that only you can know the life context, the range of associations important to you, the full sensory experience which the symbolism awakens within you. Your dream consciousness springs from deep within you - to quote Joseph Campbell once more: *"The dream is an inexhaustible source of spiritual information about yourself."* (23)

The process of journalling with the material of your dreams is incredibly valuable. This is especially so if you return to these particularly potent dreams over time, to reconsider what the dream means to you after a period of time has elapsed. Revisiting this 'Shark' dream recently has been very helpful to me - it has helped me to much more effectively put into context my response to experiences which occurred during the years following that dream.

TOWER

One of the things I have noticed after years of working with Imagery is that it has at times become a kind of short hand, a flash, like a still image from a movie, which encapsulates and communicates so much. The passage below describes an image which came to me a few months before I left Skye to live in Yorkshire.

Ironically it came as I was sitting outside in the sunshine on a magnificent early Summer's day having a cup of tea. I say ironic because the image immediately yelled 'The Tower' at me. For those who are not acquainted with it, the 'Tower' archetype in the Tarot is anything BUT an image you would associate with a quiet cup of tea in the sunshine. It usually portrays an image of destruction, most commonly of a tower being hit by lightening or perhaps being engulfed in flames. Sometimes the image is verging on violent carnage. Within the image there are often people falling from the tower. But there is one reassuring aspect which is always present in the Tower card: look at the bottom of the Tower or the structure central to the image and you will see something solid remaining at the base.

Traditional interpretations of 'The Tower' archetype often describe an experience of sudden change, usually initiated from without. The thing is, at the time the vision came to me I had already decided to leave Skye. Though incredibly emotionally charged, this decision had certainly not been imposed upon me. The change was something I was choosing and initiating myself. Fortunately I wasn't afraid of the image and so I entered into it with a little lucid dreaming. This is the result:

The scene before me is one of destruction: A stone building has collapsed, as if as a result of an earthquake. The dust is settling and all around me is eerily quiet and still. Nothing moves. I begin to walk amongst the rubble, to explore a little. I discover what had been an underground fountain of sorts, though the drains had been clogged. The force of the collapse had begun to unclog the pipes and as I watched water began to flow again, rinsing away some of the dust and accumulated grime. At the base of the fountain was a beautiful mosaic image, the tiles beginning to glisten in rich, bold colours. It looked as though it had been long forgotten; before long the beauty of this image became more and more apparent. In one corner was a dark amethyst cave lit with a thousand diamond stars; a path lead from the entrance to the cave, out then through lush woodland and to a quiet grove, where a storyteller sat, his audience entranced, his animal familiar a sleeping dragon.

I continued walking then and discovered what had been a walled garden before the collapse of the building had broken down two of the walls and most of a third. In the corner of the garden was a tree which was almost bare but for one small flower. Before the walls had collapsed the tree had been standing in almost complete shade except for the one branch which held the flower. It had stretched up into what little sunlight was available. Now the whole tree was bathed in sunlight and I couldn't help but think that before long the tree would be magnificent, in full bloom. I must admit that the flower surprised me - something so beautiful in the midst of all this rubble. I spent a little longer simply watching this flower - it seemed to awaken something in me even though I couldn't quite articulate what that may have been.

After a time I walked further, into an area which held what had been a beautifully manicured lawn. It had been so tidy before that I felt compelled to begin to move some of the rubble, to attempt to bring some sense of order to the disorder all around. As I laid out the pieces of rubble they began to form a pattern. I could see that I could, if I chose to do so, build a courtyard or a path of sorts from the pieces of rubble. I wasn't sure yet whether this was appropriate but I could picture some possibilities. So I paused - I knew I would decide in time.

I sat then amongst the rubble and noticed that the atmosphere was utterly still. The sun shone down and warmed my face - I closed my eyes then, breathed in the stillness and felt deeply peaceful.

* * * * * * *

I mentioned above that this vision came to me when I had already decided to make a significant change in my life. What I didn't anticipate was that the life I had built for myself would collapse in quite the way that it did. Leaving Skye was very painful, yet since that time I have also rediscovered dreams I had almost forgotten. Entering the vision, exploring the scene with lucid dreaming and recording it in my journal

- this has allowed me to return to it over and over again. Different aspects of this vision have stood out at different times; some of the symbols only really made sense in retrospect.

If I hadn't heeded the whisper of the Moon Hare that day I would never have uncovered the incredibly beautiful aspects hidden within the rubble. Those beautiful aspects have given me SO much reassurance over time and have reminded me over and over again of what my heart wanted to say in the midst of the busyness of life.

CHAPTER 6 - TAROT

It is a real shame that Tarot cards are so frequently associated with Fortune Telling. On the contrary I have found the Tarot to be an extraordinary tool with which to develop an independent practice of reflection, as well as a method with which to support one's interaction with the ideas and philosophies of others. The characters in the cards are familiar yet they work in a mysterious way. The stories represented in the cards operate as a kind of key to opening your own personal pathways to the imaginal world within.

ARCHETYPES

The images in a Tarot deck are archetypal. 'Archetypes' are patterns of human experience which are expressed through the language of symbols, metaphors and images. It is a framework which is not only a pattern of thoughts but more importantly, an emotional experience. Archetypes are transpersonal - beyond the personal, and are, in Jung's words:

"...Not mere names or even philosophical concepts. They are pieces of life itself - images that are integrally connected to the living individual by the bridge of the emotions." (24)

For example, 'Mother'. Every human being is born of their mother. We are each of us likely to have an extraordinary range of personal emotional experiences around our understanding of 'Mother', as well as an intellectual understanding of 'Mother' as a concept. Beyond the biological fact of motherhood, human beings of both genders have the capacity to nourish and nurture in a myriad of ways - children, animals, plants, ideas, creative projects of all types. The experience is deeply personal yet also goes way beyond that personal experience. The profound mystery of Archetypes is that they are both personal and transpersonal at the same time.

Tarot cards are particularly useful in large part because of the simple way in which they represent archetypal experiences. The characters in the Tarot are usually very clear abstractions. This makes the cards a rich resource for understanding the workings of the psyche generally, but more particularly, for understanding and integrating one's own personal experiences in life.

These beautiful yet simple images acquire meaning which each of us projects into them. And one certainly doesn't need to be a Tarot enthusiast to use the cards for personal reflection. If you have never used the Tarot start by buying yourself a deck or googling some images online. You might be a little surprised at the extraordinary variety of decks available today. This variety seems to have exploded in the last twenty years or so. There are decks which focus on particular myths and legends; woodland and fairy decks; decks based on Druidry and Wicca; decks based upon fairy tales; I have even recently encountered a deck based upon Quantum Physics!

Once you begin to get to know the cards you will notice that there are parallels in the symbolism used across decks. The paradigm or belief system of the creators of your deck/s will undoubtedly have an impact on both the artistry of the images and the interpretations the author offers. It must do. That paradigm will flow through into the images and interpretations, threading itself in ways which are sometimes subtle, sometimes quite obvious. But the archetypes upon which the cards are based form the foundations upon which the deck will be built, regardless of the paradigm of its creator/s.

Apart from the abundant variety of decks available today, there are also thousands of books and courses about reading the Tarot. It is very easy to become immersed or even a little lost in the reams of information available, especially online, about how to interpret the cards. But your own personal interaction with the cards will also tell you an enormous amount, in particular, the insight they will afford you. Insight is an incredibly powerful phenomenon - I would even go so far as to call it a grace. For this reason I have devoted a chapter to it in Part Three.

QUESTIONS

As I mentioned earlier there are many ways in which to use the Tarot - for divination; as inspiration for meditation or contemplation; in seeking to understand the motivations of others. But the way in which I have found the Tarot most useful is in reflection and journalling. These simple and often beautiful images have a way of giving your deepest heart a voice and of nudging your mind into quiet understanding.

One method of using the Tarot for reflection begins with a question. I have found over the years that these questions guide your mind into unexplored territory and lead to the most creative solutions and ideas. Clarissa Pinkola-Estes, in her book 'Women Who Run with the Wolves' explains why:

Asking the proper question is the central action of transformation-in fairy tales, in analysis and in individuation. The key question causes germination of consciousness. The properly shaped question always emanates from an essential curiosity about what stands behind. Questions are the keys that cause the secret doors of the psyche to swing open. (25)

Your question can be as simple as: "I wonder why I feel this way today?" You relax for a few moments, shuffle the cards and then select one. And then you write in your journal - you write and keep on writing, about what you see in the image, about what you feel as you look at it; you allow yourself to make associations, record memories, to notice what stands out to you in the card. And you do all of this without editing anything. Write and write and then write some more. Squeeze everything you can out of that one image. And if nothing comes to you at all, pop that card back into the deck and begin the process again with a different card.

What you uncover may be quite extraordinary, surprising, even life changing! I do not say that lightly.

More often than not though, your self knowledge will build slowly and gently, compounding over time - spirals within spirals.

Another very simple way to use the Tarot for reflection is to choose a card which appeals to you. Take a few moments to physically relax - close your eyes and take some slow deep breaths. Then turn over your cards one at a time until you find a card with which you would like to work. Consider what it is that appeals to you about this particular card. Is there some element in the card you like - an animal, the moon reflected in water, a woodland scene; perhaps a character in the card reminds you of someone you love, or of a beautiful memory. Begin writing in your journal about anything at all which comes to mind about this image. As I mentioned above, do not edit anything - simply allow yourself to jot down the thoughts, ideas and perhaps feelings that you experience as you gaze at the card.

The following is a journal note I wrote about a particular card from a deck called "Journey into the Hidden Realm" by Barbara Moore and Julia Jeffrey. The card is the 'Page of Cups'. The image shows a beautiful young woman, gently holding a silver cup, into which she is gazing. Her hair is long and dark; she has swirling blue coloured tattoos on her limbs and face; the background is dark blue; the overall tone of the card feminine and quiet.

"As I gaze at this image I am reminded of an element in 'Warming the Stone Child' by Clarissa Pinkola Estes.

Dr Estes speaks of a character from a story, a young woman who represents what she calls the 'birth of pure feeling'. I imagine that this Page has just been through a rite of passage - her tattoos are fresh and vibrant; they express her family identity as well as that which she herself has chosen. She is performing a kind of magic, warmth seeping from her hands into the liquid in her cup. She sits perfectly still - all the action is occurring within her. The water bubbles gently behind her..."

If you were to refer to a Tarot reference, or even the book which accompanies the deck from which this card comes, you would find little which is similar to what I have written above, other than perhaps the phrase 'the birth of pure feeling'. What I wrote was personal to me on that day. I hadn't asked a question; I was simply looking through the deck and was drawn to that particular card. So I followed the feeling and wrote what I felt at that time.

I cannot encourage you enough to try working with the Tarot in this way, even if you have never looked at the cards before. Even choosing a deck is a step in reflecting on what your Unconscious is communicating to you. Amid the myriad decks available, I recommend you do some research before you make your choice.

In my view no deck is superior to any other. It really is simply a matter of personal choice. By allowing your intuition a little free rein as a starting point you will begin to develop a sense of the style of cards which will suit you best. Search some Tarot images online if possible and take notice of what appeals to you. You may wish to create a 'Pinterest' board if you enjoy using that application.

Follow the links for those cards which appeal. Find out what you can about the authors and artists who have created the decks you like - this is not usually the same person. If it is possible for you to visit a bookstore which stocks Tarot cards, please do so as the images look quite different 'in the flesh' than they do in digital form.

Give yourself time in working with the cards. Try more than one deck if you can. Trust your own feelings as you look at the images in the cards rather than only relying on the interpretations offered by the author. Used in this way, the cards give you a very tangible framework with which the wise person within you can make their presence felt.

CHAPTER 7 - STORY

I have already touched upon stories in Chapter Three - Myth. What follows is one of my favourite folk stories and then some reflections about it. The story is one of the tales about the 'Selkies' or seal folk. The word 'Selkie' is the word for seal in the local dialect of the Orkney Islands in the far north of Scotland. Versions of this story are told in the frozen countries of the far north of Europe but also by the peoples of Shetland, Orkney and the Hebridean Islands off the west coast of Scotland including Skye. It was while I was living on Skye that I learned of these mythical creatures, beings who look like seals but who are able to shape-shift, to walk on land as human beings and live amongst us for a time.

Mythic tales of the sea offer a veritable kaleidoscope of imaginal characters which are dangerous, especially if they are not treated with respect. Sometimes they are even malevolent. Tales abound of seduction and misadventure of all kinds involving these creatures. If one interprets the sea motif in mythology as perhaps representing the Unconscious then entering into a dialogue with the Unconscious might be viewed as a dangerous proposition!

Selkies on the other hand are usually portrayed very much in line with their seal character - they are gentle and communal in nature and are able to enter into relationship with human beings. Most of the stories about Selkies reflect these characteristics.

The version which follows is an adaptation I have written. I have called on material from a number of sources including 'Sealskin, Soulskin' by Clarissa Pinkola Estes in her book, "Women who Run with the Wolves". (26)

SELKIE SONG

Dusk was beginning to settle, the colours of sea and sand merging. We chose a place to sit which was not too far from the fire. Daylight receded further and as if on a signal the excited chatter of families, lovers and friends began to quieten. The most gentle song then carried over the sand, so quiet at first that I could barely make it out. But it was definitely there, rising and falling with the lapping waves.

The shoreline now was indistinct and the only sounds were that of the sea, the fire and that ethereal voice.

The voice seemed to be coming from the sea itself. I was transfixed, gazing at the place where I knew the sea and sand met. And then I saw something - a dark shape which seemed to emerge from the waves. The shape moved one way then another - it seemed to expand and revolve. And then there she was! A beautiful woman, silken hair tied simply, her dress a strange mix of midnight blue and dark grey. She had been wearing a cloak which she had cast aside as she reached her place beside the fire. Now she stood perfectly still, eyes closed and she began to give full voice to the haunting song she had only hinted at until now - the Song of the Selkie.

By the time she had finished her song darkness had fallen completely - a breath-taking, clear night sky now the backdrop to her story.

* * * * * * *

Long, long ago, in the time before machines were born, there was a man who lived on a beautiful island out in the west. It was way, way out, right on the edge of the world. This man was a fisherman and he was renowned as the best of his generation. Even when the other fishermen came home grey and exhausted, dragging empty nets, he would arrive quietly, with his hold bursting.

He was certainly skilled but he was also blessed to have the village storyteller for a grandmother. His grandmother had taught him how to watch the seals – the Selkies she called them. As a boy he had passed long winters by her fire, listening to her tales, her eyes twinkling with the love she held for her Selkie friends. Watching the seals became a kind of meditation for him. He had learned how to slow his breathing and be very still and quiet, so still and quiet that his shape would merge into the rocks on the shore and he would go unseen by those beautiful, wild and wise seal eyes. He learned much from them and followed them to where the fish could always be found.

He was very eligible, this fisherman, and decided it was time that he settled down. So he made sure to be at all the ceilidhs; he danced with any number of women and was patient with all the mothers and uncles and brothers and fathers, as they introduced him to their kin. But as spring gently gave way to summer the fisherman's hopes began to dwindle into a kind of restlessness.

The days grew longer and warmer and he found it more and more difficult to sleep. A yearning loneliness had begun to take hold in his heart and though he was tired his mind refused to settle, especially in the mid-summer twilight. He began to wander out at night. He knew all the tracks, the trees and brambles, all the sudden cracks and the shale which frequently knocked others from their feet. Night after night out he would go, wandering under the stars in the strange half light, looking for… he didn't know what!

During the day he would still fish, still follow the seals, still find some echo of joy as he watched them sunning themselves, still find comfort in those wise and wild brown eyes, still smile as they would flop back into the sea with a belly laugh bark.

The year had reached mid-summer and with it one of the most important celebrations of the year. The fisherman enjoyed the noise of the music and the dancing and the laughter for a time but he could not quite shake the sense of melancholy which seemed to hang about him. He walked outside for some fresh air and when nobody was particularly taking notice he slipped quietly away.

The late night twilight was soft overhead and almost as in a dream his feet found their usual path towards the shore. The sound of the fiddles was starting up again back at the ceilidh but as he followed the path over the brow of the hill and down into the glen he could have been on a different island entirely. The silence settled around him and though he was alone he felt more at ease now that he was again sitting in one of his favourite places by the shore. It was nearing midnight and as he sat quietly, breathing in the stillness, the most beautiful full moon emerged from behind a low cloud. The fisherman's heart warmed a little with hope and his melancholy began to evaporate. Surely this was a sign - to have such a magnificent full moon right on mid-summer!

The sea was very still, a perfect mirror for the moon. As he watched the fisherman noticed those gentle tell-tale ripples which told him seals were about. In the soft glow of that moonlight those ripples opened as they always did and they appeared out of the sea - those same seal friends he had been watching since boyhood. But as they flopped onto the shore they peeled off their skins and walked, as women! The fisherman naturally couldn't believe his eyes. He hadn't had that much to drink at the ceilidh, surely. Perhaps he had 'the sight' too, like his mother, and his grandmother, and her mother before her. This was just a vision. He rubbed his eyes for a moment and then looked again…

No they were definitely still there these seal-women and they were completely naked. As he watched they walked up, up, beyond the rocks and onto a patch of flat sand. Their human skin glistened and glinted like threads of spun silk moonlight, and they danced around and around and sang in a mysterious language. Strangely he could understand their song, or he thought he could understand....at least his heart seemed to understand their song.

He couldn't move he was so entranced by what he was watching. This - this magical spectacle happening right in front of him - this was what he had been seeking, what he had been yearning for these long months of searching. The voice of his aching loneliness seemed to find an answer as he watched the Selkies' dance and listened to their enchanting song.

Time slowed. Was he asleep and in a dream? Was he awake? Had he been enchanted by some spell? He watched as the Selkies danced and danced and sang and laughed. He watched as they turned in a circle and held each others' hands, dancing a kind of magical rite with that magnificent moon watching on. Finally they ran together and threw their long arms around one another and laughed – a burst of joy, a vow of friendship and the spell was broken. It seemed to have lasted only minutes but he must have been watching for hours - the moon was reaching down to touch the sea now and the beautiful Selkies were moving again towards their home.

Creeping gently as he knew to do the fisherman moved silently towards the Selkies and without considering

what he was doing, grabbed the nearest skin and slid back behind the rocks.

The Selkies were putting on their sealskins and one by one they were slipping back into the sea, yelping and crying happily. Except for one. She kept on searching as the others began to swim away. Once the others were all again beneath the water's surface the fisherman felt emboldened and stepped from behind the rocks.

"Don't be afraid. I won't hurt you. You're so beautiful! Come with me."

"No, no I can't! Please give me my seal-skin."

"Please – you are the most extraordinary creature I have ever seen – you're everything I have been searching for. Please, come with me and be my wife and I promise I will take care of you."

"Oh I cannot be your wife," she said, " for I am of the other, the ones who live beneath."

"Be my wife," insisted the man. "I promise that in seven summers I will return your seal-skin to you and then you may stay or you may go, as you wish."

The young seal woman gazed at him with those wise brown eyes that but for her true origins, seemed human. After long silent minutes had passed she said,

"I will go with you. But at midsummer in the seventh year I must return."

* * * * * * *

In time they had a child, a beautiful boy with pale skin and dark brown eyes and in those eyes, tiny flecks the colour of silk spun silver. In winter the Selkie told the child tales of the creatures that lived beneath the sea while his father worked happily, preparing his boat and nets for spring. When his mother carried the child to bed she pointed out to the ebony skies of winter and the twilight skies of summer and the mysterious green dance of autumn. She told him stories of walrus, whale, seal and salmon and she sang him to sleep with beautiful songs of the deep sea, white sands and starry skies. And his father still walked at night, though contentedly now it seemed.

As the sixth winter began to melt into spring the beautiful Selkie began to fall ill. She lost weight and with each passing week she became a little 'less'. Her eyes became dull and she looked more and more weary. She moved more and more slowly, her joints stiffened and her sight was beginning to fade.

As mid-summer approached the little boy was awakened one night by shouting. He heard a bellowing sound such as he had never heard before. His father was yelling at his mother. And he heard a crying like bells being dropped onto rocks - his mother shouting and weeping in return! He had never heard such things.

"You hid my pelt and now the seventh mid-summer comes. You must return it to me. You promised!" cried the beautiful Selkie.

"And you woman would leave me if I gave it to you," boomed the fisherman.

"I do not know what I would do. I only know I must return to what I belong to."

The fisherman's heart was bursting, his mind was racing. He had never felt such torment, such fear! He had been so happy these past years, so content. His life had been utterly changed that mid-summer's night. He slammed open the door of the cottage and disappeared into the night. In the twilight he stormed down towards the shore and stared out to sea. It was still and calm, gently lapping as it always did on this kind of evening. He pulled aside a rock and there, still hidden after these seven years, was his Selkie wife's skin. He pushed it back between the rocks and walked off. He didn't know what to do so he did what he always did and went walking in the twilight.

The little boy loved his mother and his father but was so upset and confused by what he had heard that he cried himself to sleep. Hours passed and the cottage became deathly still and silent.

In the quiet and stillness at midnight a strange wind began to rise up from the sea, carrying with it a gentle grey mist. The boy woke and sat up. It took him a little while to realise what was happening. The wind seemed to be calling to him. Was it the wind? Or was it maybe that the wind was carrying a song? Yes – it was a song, a beautiful song and it sounded like his mother singing but it was not his mother. He really didn't understand what was happening but though the words of the song had been strange, somehow he had understood them.

He didn't know where his mother was, nor his father, but he ran out into the night anyway and towards the shore. The moon was very bright and the twilight very soft and as he watched the mist began to dissolve and he could see all the way down to the sea very clearly. And there, just for a moment, he thought he saw a seal – all that remained were the ripples. Was this where the song had been coming from?

The little boy scrambled down the path to the sea and stumbled at the bottom over a stone – no, it wasn't a stone but a bundle that had rolled out from between some rocks.

The boy opened the bundle and shook it out – it was a seal-skin! And as he held the seal-skin to his face understanding slammed through him like warm wind from the sea and instantly he knew! He just knew in his bones who his mother really was. And with that thought came another – he knew who he really was!

The little boy ran home with the sealskin flying behind him. As he burst into the cottage he found that his mother was back. Though she'd been crying she swept him and the skin up and looked deep into his eyes, and with that look she knew that he knew and understood. She scooped up the child, tucked him under her arm and half ran and half stumbled towards the sea. On the shore she pulled on her seal-skin.

"Oh mother! Don't leave me!" the little boy cried.

The beautiful Selkie paused just for a moment. She absolutely had to go back into the sea – it was as if it called to her. This urge which was mysterious and far older than she, older than time.

"I'm not going to leave you!" she cried. She took his hands looked deep into his eyes and said "You know who I am, what I am?"

"Yes" replied the little boy, very quietly.

"Then you know also where you come from?"

"Yes."

"Then close your eyes and take a very deep breath, right down to the depths of your soul."

The little boy loved and trusted his mother and so did as she had described and with that the Selkie dived with her son down into the sea.

Just at that moment the fisherman came around a bend of the shore and could only watch in despair. He cried and cried – "Oh how stupid I've been! Now I have lost them both forever."

The little boy opened his eyes and realised that he was swimming down and down with his mother and he was breathing easily under water.

The beautiful Selkie and her little boy swam deep and strong until they entered the underwater cave of seals where all manner of creatures were dining and singing, dancing and speaking, and he could understand it all!

There was such a welcome for them and a celebration that the beloved and beautiful Selkie had returned to her family and with a human child who could sing with them and breathe under water!

Seven days and nights passed during which time the lustre came back to the Selkie's hair and eyes. She turned a beautiful dark colour, her sight was restored and she began again to swim and dance and move effortlessly through the depths.

Midsummer came and it was time for the boy to return to his home – it wasn't his time to stay with his Selkie family. On that night the beautiful Selkie mother swam with her child, back up and up and up to the topside world. She placed the little boy gently on the shore in the strange twilight at midnight.

His mother hugged him and they gazed at one another, both with those soulful, wise dark eyes.

"I am always with you," she promised him. "Touch what I have touched, remember the stories and songs I taught you and you will find the song of your spirit which is both human and seal."

She hugged him for a long time but at last she tore herself away and swam out to sea. With one last long look at the boy with the beautiful brown eyes with spun silver flecks of moonlight she disappeared beneath the waters. And the little boy, because it was not his time, stayed.

The boy walked back to their cottage and found his father dozing in a chair by the window. The little boy woke his father and told him of all that he had seen and done in the world of the deep. The fisherman hugged his son and cried and laughed and cried again. He had hardly slept in those seven days, had once again been walking in the strange midsummer twilight, searching and searching the shore.

As time went on the little boy grew to be a mighty singer and storyteller and it was said this all came to be because as a child he had survived being carried out to sea by the great seal spirits.

Now, in the strange midsummer twilight, or under the magical glint of autumn's green skies, the descendants of the man he became can sometimes still be seen, sitting on a rock at the end of the sand, on the northern end of that Isle of Mists, way out in the west. His children and his children's children loved to sing and swim and they had dark brown eyes with little flecks the colour of spun-silk silver.

And there at the water's edge for a very long time afterwards there was a certain female seal who folk say would often come near the shore. And though she was a seal she looked back with those not-quite-human eyes, those beautiful wise and wild brown eyes.

* * * * * * *

The storyteller held us spellbound! She carried us with her from the joy of the Selkies dancing at midsummer, to nostalgia as the Selkie told bed-time stories to her son. Her despair at being trapped on land by her husband and her joy and exhilaration as she found her pelt and dived back into the sea.

As she finished her tale the story-teller once again stood absolutely still. And then, very softly, we heard that enchanting melody. She began to sway gently with the rise and fall of her voice and then quite magically it seemed she was cloaked again.

I suddenly became aware that I couldn't see her any more. Her voice, too, was barely discernible. And then all that was audible was the fire and the sea. Silence hung for a few more moments as if the audience didn't want to break the spell she had woven.

REFLECTIONS:

The symbolism in any folk story will offer a wealth of wisdom and guidance but especially so if it is examined in a similar manner to that with which one might analyse a dream. Philip Carr-Gomm, former head of the Order of Bards, Ovates and Druids in the United Kingdom explains:

"Instead of approaching the myth as a body of fact, disguised in a story, we need to approach it as we would a dream. Then the myth starts to breathe, starts to come alive as a story that we can enter into – a story that illuminates our own lives and purpose in the world." (27)

Just as with dreams and Tarot images, each of us has our own response to stories - our own range of associations, our own emotional responses. Stories will affect people in an extremely wide range of ways; and the same tale may affect us differently at different times in our lives. There are numerous layers of meaning. Interpretation is a deeply personal experience - my reflections on this occasion are simply a few of the myriad of possible interpretations. None is more significant than any other.

* * * * * * *

One could say that all the characters, the setting and the events in a story such as this can be interpreted as symbolic expressions of our inner world, our own psyche and our life experiences. They represent archetypal patterns.

"On a deeper level, such figures of speech reveal a greater truth than mere factual statements can deliver. Exploring how each image or action in a story can represent truths beyond the obvious yields the treasures." (28)

The geography and landscapes within which the story takes place are richly symbolic in themselves. Britain as a whole, and the islands of the far north and west of Scotland in particular, live in an intimate if somewhat contradictory relationship to the sea - as mentioned earlier a wonderful metaphor for the Unconscious. Importantly, much of the most significant action in this story takes place on the shore, a very powerful symbol for liminal space. Earth meets water; ego meets soul; conscious meets unconscious; magical creatures emerge; and in the end the little boy meets with his mother in this zone where the land meets the sea. Light, too, is a very powerful metaphor for the liminal here, as well as representing the different states of consciousness the characters experience. I was frequently beguiled by the way in which light in the Highlands tricks your perception - it is easy to understand why there have been so many tales of magical creatures emerging from this particular geographical area.

Most of the significant action also takes place at night but with a natural form of light to guide the characters in their actions. Symbolically we are shown that we are dealing with experiences playing out in the inner world but also that there will be something to guide us in doing so. Firstly the moon is the fisherman's guide; later the peculiar mid-summer twilight will show him the way. All of these allusions to light indicate that something incredibly important is occurring - he, and by extension, we, are being pushed to understand, to bring things up to conscious awareness, perhaps to awaken to a deeper sense of self-knowledge.

At other times in the tale the strange mid-summer twilight lends a dream-like quality to the action, perhaps even a sense of confusion – is the fisherman awake or asleep? The little boy, too, is dis-oriented when he hears the calling of the old seal and rushes outside to follow that call. To begin with there is mist too – how often do we hear the wise voice of guidance calling to us but we are disoriented, even fuzzy-headed in trying to understand it. The 'midnight twilight' and the light from the moon eventually allow the little boy to see, to perceive the wisdom which is calling to him and at that point he follows it passionately.

The characters and the relationships between them - the Selkie and the Fisherman and the Selkie and her son in particular, are also significant. One could interpret the Selkie as a symbol of the 'wild soul', as Clarissa Pinkola Estes describes. The child one could see as an expression of the creative spirit, arising from the marriage of the Ego (represented in the Fisherman) and the soul (represented in the Selkie). The dynamics between the characters are complex - an analysis of them could fill another book!

There are simply SO many aspects in this story which can be analysed! But there is one more particular part

upon which I would like to focus - the part in which the Selkie begins to fall ill.

The Selkie has been away for too long from her true home and from 'what she belongs to'. It is not the nature of her life on land itself which costs her so. It is the lack of replenishment to her very soul – that from which she comes. The day-to-day life we enjoy can be rich, nourishing and meaningful as well as practical. But there are times when it is not enough. We will begin to experience a diminishing of our sense of our life force if we do not nourish it with what it needs. This may be singing, or walking the dog, or learning Italian, or knitting a scarf, or walking out to see the moon at midnight – it is deeply personal and for no other purpose than we recognise that we simply must do it, whatever 'it' is, and however 'it' nourishes our soul - that deep, mysterious part of us.

We need regular access to this deeper part of ourselves, our soulful self. This is true whatever your spiritual beliefs may be, even if you consider yourself to be an atheist. If we attempt to confine or control this part of ourselves, or if we allow life or an important person in our life to do so, our sense of vitality overall will begin to diminish (29).

There is a beautiful poem by John O'Donohue, the late Irish Priest, Philosopher, Author and Poet. It is called "For One who is Exhausted: A Blessing". (I have included this poem in its entirety in the Appendix) It was sent to me by a friend during the early stages of the Covid19 pandemic, a time when the mental health challenges of lock downs were beginning to be felt, especially in the Western world.

As I read this poem at the time, it occurred to me that it acutely articulated how I perceived an adrenal burnout I experienced some years ago. After a particularly difficult period both personally and professionally, I had experienced a time of internal struggle and disenchantment which eventually tipped me into this 'burnout'. There was one particular stanza in this poem which leapt out at me: *"You have travelled too fast over false ground; Now your soul has come to take you back."*

It is the impact of a lack of soul nourishment which is highlighted so beautifully in the story of the Selkie. She neglects that deeper part of her life and she falls ill as a result. Anxiety and the phenomenon of Burnout are endemic in the Western world today. Here in this little story a light is shone right on that quiet place within and what it needs - what we all need, regardless of our spiritual beliefs.

PART THREE - GRACE

It took me quite some time to determine the title to the final Part of this book. My goal was always to explore some of the particular blessings of working with the material of one's interior world. The challenge is that the benefits of this kind of work are often difficult to quantify. At the very least, the benefits tend to evolve gently and will arise seemingly unbidden. You cannot force the Unconscious to offer up its riches on your own terms. I chose the title 'Grace' for this reason.

CHAPTER 8 - INSIGHT

One of the world's experts on the neuroscience of insight is Dr Mark Beeman. To quote Dr Beeman:

'There is a famous old quote from William James on attention: Everyone knows what attention is until you try to define it. I think a similar thing could be said about insight.' (30)

Insight is characterised by a kind of leap in the mind - there is no logical progression. Instead you experience a kind of 'knowing'. Significantly, insights involve unconscious processing. Insight seems to come from nowhere and at those times when you are not putting in a conscious effort to solve a particular problem. Have you ever had the experience of being in the shower and suddenly a solution to a problem occurs, one with which you have been wrestling for days?

That is an insight.

One of the reasons I have enjoyed using the Tarot over the years is that it is an incredibly practical way in which to access the resources of your Unconscious. What I hadn't realised for some time though, was how much working with the Tarot nurtures your capacity for Insight.

If you are someone who uses the Tarot already you will no doubt have referred to the book of interpretations which usually accompanies the cards. There is nothing wrong with that. I still do so even though I have been using the Tarot for more than twenty years. One way or another your mind stores up that information. You read and learn about the cards, building up a repertoire of interpretations. But try allowing yourself to reflect on the images themselves - let go of the interpretations of others and see what your own instinct and intuition tell you. Allow the poetry of the images to communicate directly with your Unconscious. Notice the feelings and impressions, memories, cliches and ideas, song lyrics or stories which bubble up in your mind.

Gradually, whether you realise it is happening or not, you will be working with both hemispheres of your brain, learning the interpretations of others as well as relating to the cards for yourself. This is where the magic happens! Your mind will begin to weave threads between what you have learned about the card and what you personally see in the card, merging the rational and the poetic. The edges between the two may blur - with that your experience of the wisdom encoded in the card will both expand and compound.

Focussing on the image rather than the information you have learned about the image allows your pre-frontal cortex to get out of the way. This is the part of your brain essentially responsible for conscious thought. As with any Unconscious process you cannot make an insight happen. Relax if you can. Insights are much less likely to occur when you are feeling anxious or preoccupied, or trying to solve a particular problem rationally. When you are anxious your mind and body experience a lot more overall electrical activity which makes it far more difficult for you to perceive the subtle signals your Unconscious is giving you.

"There's too much noise for you to hear well." (31)

The real magic of working with the Tarot will begin to happen as you weave between the knowledge you have gained - the things you have learned - and your dialogue with the image itself in that moment. Imagine those elements swirling around in a cauldron and then there is a flash of insight which emerges from the mixture - something new and startling and absolutely the solution you need for whatever it is you are seeking to understand, resolve or create.

Working with Imagery in all its forms opens pathways within you, but remember that you cannot control an Insight, nor any Unconscious process. I have found that Insights in particular will arise when I am not thinking about my questions.

In the final section of this chapter I would like to share an experience of just such an insight I had when I was still living on the Isle of Skye.

WARRIOR

There is a castle ruin in the far south of Skye called 'Dunscaith Castle' or 'Dun Sgathaich' (Sky-a). It is said to have been built on the ruins of a fortress built by the legendary warrior queen *Sgathaich*. Her name means 'Shadowy' in Scots Gaelic. Sgathaich appears in the Red Branch Cycle of the medieval Irish heroic legends. Cuchulainn - one of the heroes of these tales - went to Sgathaich for training. Sgathaich is one of those female

119

warriors about whom stories blur the edges between history and legend. Imagine Boudicea but with a highland accent!

Britain is an extraordinary place - the cities and many of the towns are incredibly densely populated. But there are also beautiful quiet places, often tucked out of sight. Dun Sgathaich is one of those beautiful quiet places - even visiting in summer I was often the only person there. On just such an occasion I was very relaxed, sitting in the sunshine near the castle. I found my mind wandering into that in-between liminal place, that place where logic falls away, stories unfold and flashes of insight light up in your mind's eye.

It was then that I had an image of Sgathaich herself standing before me. I have a number of Tarot decks in which the figure portrayed in the Strength card is a woman, and in a couple in particular, this archetype is called 'The Warrior'. This is how Sgathaich appeared to me - a Celtic warrior, strong, confident, relaxed, holding up her sword, its blade glinting in the sunlight. In that moment I somehow knew that this sword image encapsulated one's sense of identity, that deeper self-knowledge, potential and strength which lies within each and every one of us.

The Celtic warrior was understood to be the 'bringer of the new age' - the person who had the courage to enter unknown territory. In Mythic terms of course this isn't geographical territory. Rather it is new territory in *life* - new experiences, new people, new skills. Knowing oneself, one's deepest heart, the sense of one's strengths - this is what equips you to break new ground, try new things, meet new people. It is this internal strength which equips you to do so.

Did I simply imagine Sgathaich to be standing there? Possibly. Perhaps in my relaxed state I accessed a form of internal guidance - an 'Inner Advisor' as it is sometimes known to psychologists. Is Dun Sgathaich - the place - infused with a special kind of energy, a *genius loci*? Well in my opinion, yes! The point is it doesn't really matter. What matters is that I came away that day with an insight about identity, an insight which has been incredibly helpful to me and to others with whom I have worked over the years since.

CHAPTER 9 -
SOUL NOURISHMENT

I have called this chapter 'Soul Nourishment' so before I go any further I must explain what I mean by the term 'Soul', albeit without entering too far into semantics. Throughout this book I have written about the mysterious world we each hold within - our deepest sense of who we are in our heart of hearts. This is a part of our being which is often neglected in the rush and busyness of life. It is the part of us which I believe craves nourishment, regardless of whether we hold particular spiritual beliefs or not. It is the mysterious essence of who we are and out of which our own unique life emerges. This is how I, personally, understand 'soul'.

One's 'Spirituality' I would describe as one's 'Cosmology' - our world view, beliefs and contemplative practices, rather than one's 'Religion'.

Indeed there seems to be enormous scope in the way in which people express their sense of Spirituality or spiritual identity today. This is not really surprising, given that during the last 50 years or so in the Western world we have witnessed enormous change in religious observance and spiritual practice. Traditional Christian churches have seen a profound reduction in their congregations - much of Western culture now is secular, at least on the surface. There has been a trend in the West too of people turning to Eastern spiritual traditions, even if in some cases it is in a diluted, simplistic form. The so-called 'New Age' movement with its eclectic mix of esoteric beliefs grew enormously during the 1970s and has continued to do so since, incorporating practices from Spiritualism to Mind-Body holistic healing practices and beyond. Druidry, Wicca and a range of Neo-Pagan beliefs have become almost mainstream in their adherence.

Against this backdrop there has been another phenomenon - the development of a group of people who these days identify themselves as 'Spiritual but not Religious'. This group is growing year by year in the West. By way of example: Professor Michael King from University College London concluded in 2013 that approximately 20% of the population of the United Kingdom fit into this category. In the United States a survey in 2017 concluded that almost 20% of Americans now consider themselves as being interested in spiritual matters, even though they never step inside a church, a temple or a synagogue.

Dr Lionel Corbett is a psychiatrist and Jungian analyst who specialises in Depth Psychology. (Depth psychology is a field of study which explores how the unconscious aspects of the human experience influence psychological conditions and treatment.) In his book 'Psyche and the Sacred' Dr Corbett suggests that the sacred cannot be defined - we can only talk about how we experience it. It is the quality of one's experience, its numinous, awe-inspiring quality which demonstrates its sacred nature rather than the structure and doctrine of an established religion. (32) If one accepts this notion then the continuing growth of this 'Spiritual but not Religious' group is not at all surprising.

I would say that I, too, belong to this 'Spiritual but not Religious' group, though I tend to resist defining my own spiritual beliefs too strictly. Those beliefs are grounded in Celtic Paganism but I am also inspired by the understandings of the Perennial tradition - the wisdom inherent in all spiritual paths and teachings. Developing what is mostly an independent and autonomous contemplative practice has been extremely important to me - it suits me very well. I do not mind admitting though that I searched for a long time before I came to the sense of peacefulness I now experience in that contemplative practice. Sadly, I have found through that process of searching that there are an enormous number of people who assume what I can only call an inflated sense of 'spiritual authority', and especially so in the digital arena.

Working with Imagery has been an incredibly significant part of the process I worked through to discover that peacefulness. It is Imagery in its various forms which has guided me to the wisdom which would support me the most, including the particular wisdom to which we all have access - the wisdom which arises from within.

'Wisdom' like 'Truth' is not absolute. It is mysterious and one's experience of it is completely subjective. In the absence of regular (more conventional) religious rituals, a contemplative practice of reflection and journaling with Imagery at its core has been incredibly enriching for me.

I am using the term 'Contemplation' deliberately, even though some might consider it to be quite an old-fashioned term, like 'convalescence' or even 'community'. When I mention contemplation, I am not referring to simply 'thinking about' things.

The contemplative practice I recommend requires a certain kind of state of mind, one in which you can muse, daydream, imagine, journal, reflect, and then perhaps plan and set some goals. It is the state of mind which allows you to let go of time, to access that quiet wisdom within. This is the case whether you have a particular spiritual belief or practice, or not.

Working with Imagery in such a contemplative prac tice over time helps you to build a repertoire of symbols which are important to you. You will uncover pathways into your own internal landscape and gradually get to know how your Unconscious likes to communicate with your conscious mind.

I explained in the Preface why I chose the image of the 'Moon Hare' for the title of this book. For me, this mythical creature encapsulates how the voice of my own Unconscious speaks. It is almost always quiet, gentle and subtle. I notice something bubbling up into awareness and if I am not careful, it disappears before I have been able to really understand its message. I quoted Alan Lightman in Chapter One, where he describes the breathing of his spirit:

"Those breaths are so tiny and delicate". (33)

I mentioned in a previous chapter too that I experienced an Adrenal Burnout some years ago. Long before I tipped into that burnout though, my Unconscious had been trying to let me know that there was something radically wrong.

The Unconscious is an extraordinary thing - it whispers to you in all sorts of ways. When I was at my busiest (ironically whilst I was running a Retreat Centre on Skye) I would find myself writing articles inspired by 'The Hermit' archetype in the Tarot. I would light my own lantern and have candles burning on my desk, even in the middle of the day. I would fantasise about the time when I would be able to rest properly - to keep the blinds drawn, put on some gentle music and shut out the world for a while. After leaving Skye I did eventually have the luxury of cocooning myself in my new home in North Yorkshire. I understood by then very clearly what I needed in order to heal both my physical and my mental health.

The thing is, the Hermit had been trying to tell me that for some time - that image was pointing me to exactly what I needed had I only noticed it at the time.

It had also been trying to point me to a crucial facet of this archetype which I didn't really understand until much later - the aspect of 'soul nourishment'. There is no doubt that unacknowledged stress and over-work played a significant part in my adrenal burnout. But I believe that a prolonged lack of soul nourishment was the most damaging part of all.

Working with Imagery in all its forms, becoming comfortable with entering the Mythic Imagination, has changed my understanding of myself and of those whom I love. It is a wonderful way in which to cultivate a healthy sense of self-awareness and one's deeper identity. Each of the Imaginal pathways discussed in this book will guide you inwards and will support you to seek out your own well of insight and wisdom.

What I have shared though is only my experience of working with it. I apologise if that sounds obvious. The truth is that cultivating a personalised contemplative practice can be a bit of a balancing act, between learning from others whose wisdom and perspective you respect and with whom you resonate, and listening to your own internal wisdom.

In this book I have focused on the latter. There is no doubt that I have learned a great deal from authors and teachers whom I respect enormously. Their wisdom and insight have been invaluable to me. My focus here has been on one's own personal gateways to wisdom. That does not diminish what I have learned from others nor do I perceive one to be superior to the other. This process though does require a fundamental trust in oneself. In Chapter Two I briefly discussed Jung's concept of the 'Collective Unconscious'. We each have our own connections with this mysterious world - each 'pathway' in this book will guide you to those connections, those gateways. When you explore your own interior world, remember that it is constantly being nourished by that mysterious 'collective' realm. What emerges from your Unconscious doesn't necessarily come just from you, from your Ego identity - the experience we each have of being a separate person with our own mind and our own subjective experience of the world. You are likely to be touched by something truly inspiring.

The blessings which arise as a result of exploring one's interior world can be nothing short of extraordinary. Here is where a kind of magic happens - synchronicities, brilliant flashes of insight which seem to arise spontaneously within you, real wisdom which touches your heart as well as your mind and which inspires joyfully creative ideas - solutions to previously insurmountable problems. Sometimes you may just notice a hint of recognition, an intuition which whispers to you or nudges you to further exploration or study.

I would like to conclude by turning once again to Joseph Campbell. In '*Pathways to Bliss*', he shares something he learned from his mentor Heinrich Zimmer, namely that the best things cannot be explained - they are transcendent and are inexpressible truths. The second best are myths which are metaphoric attempts to point the way to the first. He then shares a quote from '*The Quest for the Holy Grail*', an Arthurian story written in the 13th century by an anonymous monk.

"They thought it would be a disgrace to go forth in a group. Each entered the Forest Adventurous at that point which he himself had chosen, where it was darkest and there was no way or path." (34)

Trusting one's own internal world is fundamental to unlocking the riches of the Unconscious and the grace which it offers. Understanding the language of Imagery, however it is expressed, opens infinite pathways into the source of those riches, to the wisdom and creativity which arise from within.

END NOTES:

1. MacKellar, Dorothea: *My Country. 1908*
2. Pinkola-Estes, Clarissa: *Warming the Stone Child. Myths and Stories about Abandonment and the Unmothered Child. 1990*
3. Larsen, Stephen: *The Mythic Imagination. 1990*
4. O'Donohue, John: *The Four Elements. 2011*
5. Larsen, Stephen: *The Mythic Imagination. 1990*
6. Rossman, Martin: *Guided Imagery for Self-Healing. 2000*
7. Berry, Wendell: *The Peace of Wild Things. 2018*
8. Lightman, Alan: *In Praise of Wasting Time. 2018*
9. Campbell, Joseph: *The Power of Myth. 1988*
10. O'Donohue, Pat: *Quoted in The Four Elements. 2011*
11. Hesse, Hermann: *Siddhartha. 1922*
12. Campbell, Joseph: *The Power of Myth. 1988*
13. Carr-Gomm, Philip: *Druid Mysteries - Ancient Wisdom for the 21st Century. 2002*
14. Matthews, John: *The Celtic Shaman - A Practical Guide. 1991*
15. Yorke, John: *Into the Woods. 2014*
16. Young, Jonathan: *SAGA - Best New Writings on Mythology. Volume 1. 1996*
17. Ibid
18. Schulman, Tom: *Dead Poets Society. 1989*
19. Campbell, Joseph: *Pathways to Bliss. Mythology and Personal Transformation. 2004*
20. Wikipedia
21. Price, Nancy: *Acquainted with the Night - A Book of Dreams. 1949*
22. Pinkola-Estes, Clarissa: *Women who Run with the Wolves. 1989*
23. Campbell, Joseph: *The Power of Myth. 1988*
24. Jung, Carl G: *Man and his Symbols. 1964*
25. Pinkola-Estes, Clarissa: *Women who Run with the Wolves. 1989*

26. Ibid
27. Carr-Gomm, Philip: *Druid Mysteries - Ancient Wisdom for the 21st Century. 2002*
28. Young, Jonathan: *SAGA - Best New Writings on Mythology. Volume 1. 1996*
29. Pinkola-Estes, Clarissa: *Women who Run with the Wolves. 1989*
30. Beeman, Mark: *Quoted in Your Brain at Work by David Rock. 2009*
31. Ibid
32. Corbett, Lionel: *Psyche and the Sacred. 2006*
33. Lightman, Alan: *In Praise of Wasting time. 2018*
34. Campbell, Joseph: *Pathways to Bliss. Mythology and Personal Transformation. 2004*

APPENDIX

Dorothea McKellar

The love of field and coppice,
Of green and shaded lanes.
Of ordered woods and gardens
Is running in your veins,
Strong love of grey-blue distance
Brown streams and soft dim skies
I know but cannot share it,
My love is otherwise.

I love a sunburnt country,
A land of sweeping plains,
Of ragged mountain ranges,
Of droughts and flooding rains.
I love her far horizons,
I love her jewel-sea,
Her beauty and her terror -
The wide brown land for me!

A start white ring-barked forest
All tragic to the moon,
The sapphire-misted mountains,
The hot gold hush of noon.
Green tangle of the brushes,
Where lithe lianas coil,
And orchids deck the tree-tops
And ferns the warm dark soil.

Core of my heart, my country!
Her pitiless blue sky,
When sick at heart, around us,
We see the cattle die -
But then the grey clouds gather,
And we can bless again
The drumming of an army,
The steady, soaking rain.

Core of my heart, my country!
Land of the Rainbow Gold,
For flood and fire and famine,
She pays us back threefold -
Over the thirsty paddocks,
Watch, after many days,
The filmy veil of greenness
That thickens as we gaze.
An opal-hearted country,
A wilful, lavish land -
All you who have not loved her,
You will not understand -
Though earth holds many splendours,
Wherever I may die,
I know to what brown country
My homing thoughts will fly.

THE PEACE OF WILD THINGS
Wendell Berry

When despair for the world grows in me
and I wake in the night at the least sound
in fear of what my life and my children's
lives may be, I go and lie down where the wood drake
rests in his beauty on the water, and the great hero
feeds

I come into the peace of wild things
who do not tax their lives with forethought
of grief. I come into the presence of still water.
And I feel above me the day-blind stars
waiting with their light. For a time
I rest in the grace of the world, and am free.

DOLPHIN MAGIC

Jessica sat bolt upright in bed, sweat trickling, heart pounding. The blanket of darkness and silence disoriented her. She must have cried out in her sleep again - Milo was looking up from his bed in the corner, alert, ready to spring towards any threat. She turned on a light, reassured him, pulled on her robe and went to make tea. She stood with her eyes closed, barefoot, the cool of the kitchen tiles refreshing. It took a few long, drawn out minutes for her mind to clear and for her pulse to slow. The morning rituals helped. The simple regular movements instilled a sense of calm. She went to sit in her favourite chair, as she did most mornings, looking out at the sea. Her life had always revolved around the sea: hobbies, study, work, refuge.

It had been the same dream, the one that had come at least three times before.

This dream was so terrifying that Jess had begun to have difficulty getting to sleep. As if the stress of the last year wasn't enough, now she had begun to feel decidedly sleep deprived.

It always began the same way. It was a beautiful, warm summer's day, and she was walking along the jetty at the island marina where her parents had kept their little boat. Something would catch her eye, a glint of sunlight on water. She would lean over to look into the clear depths of the bay and then the shark would leap out, perfectly vertical, just as dolphins do, except for the rows and rows of its teeth.

That much had been the same each time she'd had the dream. And she would wake up at exactly the same point – just as the shark was leaping out of the water. She'd wake as she had this morning – abruptly, her heart pounding.

This time though, something else had happened in the dream. As the shark had leapt out, she had dived into the water on the other side of the jetty and she had immediately become a seal – perfect food for a shark. What on earth went on in her unconscious?

It surprised Jess that in the dream she could move through the water faster than she had ever moved in her life. And she could see perfectly in that alternative world. The colours were extraordinarily vibrant and the water was clear, cool, and teeming with life. All around her were at least a dozen other seals, and dolphins, all swimming incredibly fast, forming a kind of body-guard around her. The shark was still there behind them and seemed to be gaining speed. She was sure she could feel its presence almost upon her. But this was also her territory. She knew where she was going and she knew how to manoeuvre, just enough to keep out of the shark's reach. After what seemed like an eternity she felt the sand beneath her and she flopped up onto the beach of the mainland. Miraculously she stood up as a woman again and turned to look out at that beautiful water; relieved, exhausted and thrilled to witness the end of the chase. It was at this point in the dream that she had woken up today, her heart still racing but this time from the exhilaration of her escape rather than from abject terror.

She got up from her chair now, the clarity of her dream firing up a kind of determination to get on with the day, this very important day. Today was her day in court, the day when she would finally face the predator who had inspired so many tears and sleepless nights, so many drunken late night phone calls to her brother. She had dreaded this day for months, until now. Now the clarity of her dream inspired her. She stretched, her mind calm and her heart hopeful, for the first time in almost a year.

She moved quickly through the morning then, showering, dressing, driving into the city. As she walked into court to meet her barrister she saw her opponent. He was sitting calmly, wearing his very expensive grey suit, with his very expensive lawyer beside him, looking, as always, calmly arrogant. He knew that the whole world would simply choose to get out of his way.

For the first time since it began Jessica felt completely relaxed. She looked at him and in her minds' eye she remembered the end of her dream. When she had stood up on that beach she could see the shark's fin turning to head back out into deeper water. What the shark hadn't noticed was the pod of dolphins surging towards it, ready to pound into it with their blunt snouts. The shark's body floating on the surface of the sea was the last thing she remembered as she had woken this morning.

Dolphins are one of the only creatures that can kill a shark – clearly her arrogant predator didn't know that. She calmly looked over at him, returned and held his gaze. Normally she would avoid looking him in the eye but not this time. This time he couldn't intimidate her. Her barrister had said that she had a great case and that rarely did anyone take this man to court. Normally he would manipulate, bully or threaten anyone whose business he wanted to take over.

Finally Jess looked away and she couldn't stop the hint of a smile dancing about her lips. Then she looked down at her papers, at the triangle of dolphins that comprised her logo and in that moment she knew that she was going to win.

FOR ONE WHO IS EXHAUSTED, A BLESSING
by John O'Donohue

When the rhythm of the heart becomes hectic,
Time takes on the strain until it breaks;
Then all the unattended stress falls in
On the mind like an endless, increasing weight.

The light in the mind becomes dim.
Things you could take in your stride before
Now become laborsome events of will.

Weariness invades your spirit.
Gravity begins falling inside you,
Dragging down every bone.

The tide you never valued has gone out.
And you are marooned on unsure ground.
Something within you has closed down;
And you cannot push yourself back to life.

You have been forced to enter empty time.
The desire that drove you has relinquished.
There is nothing else to do now but rest
And patiently learn to receive the self
You have forsaken in the race of days.

At first your thinking will darken
And sadness take over like listless weather.
The flow of unwept tears will frighten you.
You have traveled too fast over false ground;
Now your soul has come to take you back.

Take refuge in your sense, open up
To all the small miracles you rushed through.

Become inclined to watch the way of rain
When it falls slow and free.

Imitate the habit of twilight,
Taking time to open the well of colour
That fostered the brightness of day.

Draw alongside the silence of stone
Until its calmness can claim you.
Be excessively gentle with yourself.

Stay clear of those vexed in spirit.
Learn to linger around someone of ease
Who feels the have all the time in the world.

Gradually, you will return to yourself,
Having learned a new respect for your heart
And the joy that dwells far within slow time.

Lightning Source UK Ltd.
Milton Keynes UK
UKHW010643111122
411977UK00004B/21